# DEAR

## Wife

**A WIFE LIKE ME**

Contributor Team founded by

Amanda Davison

# What people are saying about
# DEAR *Wife*

"The authors of *Dear Wife* masterfully meet wives right where they are with beautifully-written and heartfelt stories of struggle and hope. They help wives to see Jesus at work in every one of their letters, and they invite wives into a deeper connection with Jesus and their husbands like a sweet friend reaching out across the table to grab your hand and pray with you. *Dear Wife* is truly a must-read for every wife who wants to grow in the Lord and in her marriage. You'll love it!"

**Ashley Willis**, co-author of *The Naked Marriage*

"Hey wives! You already said "I do." This book is a fresh new way to say, "I will." The amazing women who wrote this book are just like you—they are wives who wanted to find meaning and connection in their marriages. And that's exactly what they found. And now, they are giving you practical, Biblical steps to grow closer to your husbands, and most importantly, to God."

**Jennifer Dukes Lee**, author of *It's All Under Control* and *The Happiness Dare*

"Marriage is beautiful, and marriage is hard. We know this. But how often do we stop to consider how marriage is God's idea? In this profoundly meaningful book, an insightful team of real-life authors—wives like you and me—remind us that our earthly relationships are inextricably tied to our heavenly relationships, and that knowing Jesus means knowing and loving our husbands on a deeper level. Relatable, encouraging, and solidly biblical, *Dear Wife* is a remedy for every marriage that needs to reconnect with God and one another. I will revisit these pages again and again."

**Becky Kopitzke**, author of *Generous Love* and *The Cranky Mom Fix*

"As a pastor in ministry for over 20 years, I have seen the trajectory of marriages spiral when a husband and wife lose connection with Christ and with one another. And it happens in that order. *Dear Wife* is a call to remember, reconnect with, and remain in the One who resources our life and our marriage. Apart from Him, we can do nothing. Amanda and the *A Wife Like Me* team share their stories of self-induced failure and God's faithfulness in marriage with refreshing honesty, humor, and humility. In so doing, they point us directly to Jesus who holds all things together, including your marriage."

**Clay Mitchell**, Lead Pastor at The Naz

"Wife, if you wrestle with feeling disconnected you are not alone. *Dear Wife* is a wonderful collection of *real* women sharing *real* answers to help you rekindle connection with your husband—and with your Heavenly Father."

**Rhonda Stoppe**, No Regrets Woman, author of
*The Marriage Mentor* and *Real Life Romance*

"*Dear Wife* is a wonderful road map for any woman wanting to find her way back to feeling 'loved' by her husband. It's deep, practical and easy to read. Any woman feeling lonely within her marriage would benefit greatly by reading this book."

**Matt Loehr**, President, Dare to be Different, and Director of
Marriage Mentoring: Love and Respect

"If you are looking for your marriage to grow, this is your devotional. You will be challenged, you will be convicted, and you will be loved in the process. I've read lots of marriage devotional books and after a few days, they start to collect dust. This will not be your experience as you read *Dear Wife*. Amanda and her *A Wife Like Me* team are transparent in their own marriages and they offer sound, practical, tangible tools to connect with God and your husband. I loved reading the invitations, because they were timely and achievable, and yet, they challenged me to think about my marriage differently throughout my day."

**Melissa Clark**, MA, LPC-S, Christian Counselor
for Individuals, Couples, and Teens

"*Dear Wife* was literally dropped into my inbox at a time when I wanted nothing to do with being a wife. I was tired and weary and part of me was ready to give up. I had, only weeks before diving into it's content, thrown my hands up in despair in yet another hard argument with my husband of 8 years. Forever seemed too long. As I somewhat reluctantly dove into the words penned on the pages of *Dear Wife*, that were clearly written for other women, I found myself floored by my response. My heart was softening, awakening, to a concept much greater than myself; the love and servanthood of our Jesus. *Dear Wife* is not just for failing marriages, succeeding marriages, wives of 2 days or 55 years. It's for us all, all of us in the trenches of living lives as wives in today's cultural climate. The structure of *Dear Wife* is helpful and practical with great application and calls to action in each chapter. I highly recommend this book to married women of all ages and stages. There's something for every wife in the pages of this well written book."

**Chrystan Ferrell**, author and speaker

"After being a wife for five years, I don't know anything worth investing in more than my relationship with Jesus and my husband. If you're hoping to develop a more intimate, joyful relationship with your spouse, *Dear Wife* is the book to help you do just that."

**Lauren Gaskill**, author, speaker and president of *She Found Joy*

"Amanda gets wives. And she knows how to reveal a deeper side to life's most common trials. In *Dear Wife* Amanda and her team beautifully share encouragements to wives of all ages that will spark a deeper connection with God and their husband. With frankness and compassion, readers will find a safe place to expose their burdens and find themselves healed."

**Denise Pass**, speaker, worship leader and author of *Shame Off You* and *31 Days to Hope Reinvented*

"This book is real encouragement written by real women in real marriages, with real faith in Christ. Without painting pictures of rainbows and butterflies, these women share relatable stories from their own lives, providing practical application based on the examples we see from Jesus in scripture. I heartily recommend this read for any wife who is looking to build connection with Jesus or with her husband, because with this book you'll get both! Thank you, *A Wife Like Me*, for this wonderful tool for connection!"

**Amy Garvin**, wife and mom, and professional receiver of grace

Printed in the United States of America

First printing 2019

Cover and interior book design by Emily Weigel

ISBN: 978-0578470597

Published by A Wife Like Me
www.awifelikeme.com

*For all the wives.*

# Contents

# DEAR *Wife,*

I hear you. I hear your sigh of exhaustion from work and preparation. Of grabbing groceries, of emotional soothing, of never-ending discipline. I hear your aching for rest and for connection. I hear your heart cries, spoken and unspoken.

I see you. I see your attempts to live your ideal life. To be healthier. Softer, more patient, and more joy-filled. I see your efforts to make your marriage better. The encouragement, direction, desire to please, guilt, and remarks—all intended to bring you somewhere better than where you are. I see your heart, longing for real intimacy with your husband.

I know you. I know your thoughts: wishing your marriage felt less like roommates and more fulfilling and alive, wanting to not be taken for granted. Wishing you had more time with your husband, wondering how you can keep it all balanced, wanting to not feel alone.

I am extending the ultimate invitation to a journey of fresh connection with Me, because a thriving relationship with your husband begins with a thriving relationship with Me. I desire to walk intimately with you in new ways. I long for you to let me into the deepest areas of your heart. I hope for uninterrupted connection with you. Through these pages, you'll see how real connection is built and experience it for yourself. This journey will challenge, grow, and mature your deepening connection with Me and with your husband. I can't wait, sweet wife.

With the greatest love,
Your Number One (Jesus)

# A Word of Caution

Many well-meaning Christian marriage books offer great wisdom and help to marriages that are healthy but in need of a tune-up. These books are also potentially helpful for marriages that are in a difficult season or where there is turmoil. However, what is helpful for the marriages just described can be harmful for marriages where there is any type of abuse, addiction, or abandonment.

This book is geared toward wives who are looking to enhance their marriage, for wives who might be in a difficult season in their marriage, or in a marriage relationship where the wife feels disconnected from her husband. But please know, there is a difference between a difficult yet healthy marriage (just described), and a dysfunctional, destructive marriage where there is any type of abuse, addiction, or abandonment. Of these two types of marriages, the tools offered in this book are geared toward the former—not the latter.

If you wonder whether your marriage might be unhealthy, we recommend reading Leslie Vernick's *The Emotionally Destructive Marriage*. We also recommend seeking the help of a professional counselor to help you walk through any issues of abuse and to begin your specific journey of healing.

No matter where you are in your journey as a wife, know that you are loved, and there is nothing you can do about it. You are loved by a Mighty God, and there is nothing you ever have done or will do that could change His love for you.

# Introduction

I didn't need anything more than I did that day in 2001, lying on the floor of his bedroom, pillow shoved over my face. The force of his body over mine was too much, and my fight was leaving me. I was unable to comprehend how this could have happened and instead had only one thought—that this might be the end for me.

It wasn't the end. In fact, little did I know it was just one more battle I'd face in a day of reckoning that would arrive much later, in 2012.

This high school boyfriend turned college boyfriend served an important role in my life at that time: he loved me. I hadn't felt special before he came along. So although the relationship was unhealthy because neither of us was healthy—me with an unhealthy desperation to be loved and he, abusing drugs and alcohol—I stayed. Because when we don't know the love of the Father, we'll do almost anything to experience it through people.

When I arrived at his apartment to announce the end of our relationship, he had just used. And for the first time in our relationship—the last time he'd ever touch me—he physically hurt me. He didn't want me to leave him.

But as I lay there wondering why he was harming me, as painful as it was, I was faced with the sobering realization that this man couldn't provide the love I longed for. Another dead end. My earlier relationship flings, my experimenting with drugs, and own abuse of alcohol all had turned up empty. And now he was, too.

Shifts and changes, as painful as they can be, are what awaken our hearts to something new. The police forcing their way into that third-floor apartment and finding me in the room was one small slit of many that tore open my heart, one that would later bring me to a place of receiving and accepting the greatest offer of my life.

I never want to minimize the process of pain. The longing of our hearts for life to be different. The experience of disappointment, of unmet hopes or unlived dreams. I don't want to diminish the long fight for restoration, for health, or for stronger relationships. Because these are all important pieces in our becoming undone. Each of them furthers our individual process to opening the greatest personal invitation we will ever receive.

I'll admit that I never fully understood how each painful piece of my own life specifically served a purpose until working on this book. Being on this side of life in Christ, I knew they were part of the full story of surrendering my life to Him, but I couldn't put the pieces together until now.

My undoing was hard and painful.

I believed at a young age that I would be a counselor, one who helped married couples. I wanted to help couples better understand each other and find ways to live happily in their marriage. So I went to college and then started graduate school. At the same time I was in graduate school, I was also married with a young daughter and newborn son. I learned great tools and techniques to help married couples during school, yet as I began to apply them to my own marriage, I became increasingly frustrated with how they only helped for a short period of time. Realizing that my strategies weren't working, my irritation grew, and I tried other ways of getting my husband to change. I would try to make my husband feel guilty, shame him, disrespect him, give him the cold shoulder, or withhold love from him. You name it, I tried it—all in an effort for him to love me more or love me better.

But it seemed like the harder I tried, the worse our relationship got.

One day, it all came crashing down. I had poured so much energy into making my marriage great and getting my husband to love me that when he came home late on a day that was important to me, I put on an Academy Award-worthy performance. Standing by the door holding our newborn, words erupted out of me as soon as he entered the house. I declared that my fight was over. I told him that we could not be married if he would not show me more love. I took our two children and stormed out of the house with him following. Years of my pleading hadn't gotten through to him. His confusion in the face of my fury angered me even more. I didn't know it at the time, but this good man who loved me so well would never be able to live up to the God-sized expectations I had been placing on him.

I slammed the car doors shut and drove off. Weeping hysterically, I only made it across the highway to where our farm shop was located. I parked the car and wept. Left without any other options of my own, I cried out to God for answers.

Even as I wept over the situation with my husband, I had a flashback to that awful day, years earlier, when I lay on the floor with the pillow over my face. As it flashed before me, I became even angrier. My tears were uncontrollable. *Why, God? Why all of these hard things? Why me? Why is it that I've had to endure confusion, loss, and illness? Why do I feel unworthy of being loved? Why can't my husband love me more? Why isn't he changing? Why isn't this working? I'm done. I'm so tired of trying.*

I've since realized that it is in moments like these that we become beautifully undone. In these raw moments with God, where I finally looked to Him for answers and direction, I saw that He had been holding out an invitation all along. I had just never emptied myself out enough to see it, open it, accept it, and respond to it. Realizing that I was the one blocking myself from experiencing the life and love I had always wanted was the final tear in the envelope that I needed to open and enter into God's invitation for my life and marriage.

What happened in the year that followed was nothing short of a miracle. God brought this stubborn, strong-willed, fiery girl to her knees in surrender, showed me that there is no other way to live in fullness and in freedom other than through and with Him, and demonstrated that there is a great promise for all who respond to His invitation.

I see now that each difficult milestone in my life was a tear in the envelope of the letter God had written to me, holding it in my heart. Each time pain from others and from the personal decisions I made ripped my heart open, it also ripped open yet another piece of the envelope holding His letter inside. Short-lived, painful experiences served as small tears; others were deep and long-lasting, producing slow and ongoing distress. The larger tears did the most damage, even as they opened up the envelope in wider segments.

All painful experiences matter. They all play a part in the undoing of our souls and the process of opening the greatest, most personal invitation we've ever received.

Friend, there is a great invitation waiting for you, too. This letter of invitation is the same for each of us, yet it is unique as well. It is the same in that it is personal: God has invited each of us, by name, into relationship with Him. His invitation is not written anonymously but is meant specifically for you. This invitation is personal because God knows you. He formed you and has a plan for you. This invitation is also intimate, inviting you into a new, deeper place of connection with Him because He cares for you. Your invitation is written with hopeful expectation, because the Writer desires you to use your free will to answer the invitation. He waits for your response. Your invitation is also exciting, because it is an open door for you to dwell with God and join Him on a daily journey of new life.

What if God is asking you to rip open the envelope tucked into your heart and accept His invitation? What if He has led you to this very moment, to the decision to lay it all out for Him to grab hold? What if you chose to stop white-knuckling your life, your family, and your marriage, and instead lived in freedom? What if you chose to expose your weakest and most ugly self—your inclination toward self-preservation, self-defense, and selfishness—to finish tearing the envelope, once and for all? What if you decided to be done living a half-full life, giving God what only feels safe, and instead chose to trust God with all of it? What if you surrendered your life, your marriage, and your children to God's control? What if you said "yes" to Christ today?

I pray you will, friend. I pray that you will review your life so far and see each moment of frustration, pain, disappointment, or trauma as tears that have slowly been opening your personal invitation from God. If you haven't fully ripped open the envelope, I pray you do now. I pray you break apart anything that has held you back from a real relationship with Christ and give Him full access and control of your life. I pray you lay it all at God's feet, surrendering everything to Him. He can handle it. He will use it. He can be trusted. Be done with living a held-back life, not fully free. It's time.

Your personal invitation includes three questions and is very short.

> Dear Wife,
> Will you follow me?
> Will you trust me?
> Will you try it my way?
>
> Expectantly,
> Your Father

What is your response to such an invitation?

If you have not yet chosen to follow Christ, I pray that now would be your time. Maybe you've never been down on the floor, feeling hurt or ashamed. But maybe you've felt hopeless, restless, or without joy. Maybe you're tired of trying hard with little results. Wife, your Heavenly Father loves you so much that He sent His Son to pay the penalty of brokenness, so that we would not live without hope for our eternal future or lack hope, freedom, and joy in our current life. Your Heavenly Father loves you so much that nothing you ever have done, are doing, or could do would change His love for you. It is a love that makes no sense to us, because our love is not capable of the love He shows. Yet it is His magnificent love that transforms us and resides within those who believe in Him, helping us as believers to grow in our capacity to love.

No matter where you are in your faith journey, I pray that you would take this opportunity to commit or recommit your life to Christ, so that everything that happens from this moment forward would be for Him and done through Him.

### The Sinner's Prayer (by Dr. Ray Pritchard)

*Lord Jesus, for too long I've kept you out of my life. I know that I am a sinner and that I cannot save myself. No longer will I close the door when I hear you knocking. By faith I gratefully receive your gift of salvation. I am ready to trust you as my Lord and Savior. Thank you, Lord Jesus, for coming to earth. I believe you are the Son of God who died on the cross for my sins and rose from the dead on the third day. Thank you for bearing my sins and giving me the gift of eternal life. I believe your words are true. Come into my heart, Lord Jesus, and be my Savior. Amen.[1]*

All of heaven erupts with celebration when you accept the invitation from God to dwell with Him. He is our home and our safe place. If I could reach through these words right now, I would hug you, cry happy tears, and share in the joy of our King. It begins here—with you and with me. But it doesn't end here. This is just the beginning for us, which excites me to no end. This invitation from God to join Him is a daily, ongoing invitation that requires a daily, ongoing response. It's a response of continued trust, an inner "yes" to relinquish our self-deceit of self-sufficiency. It's a decision to again and again withdraw our self-protection and abandon control. His invitation to us to trust Him throughout each day is one that provides overwhelming peace amidst daily, real struggles. Please know, friend, that opportunities where we want to control the outcome are places where we have the most potential for growth. Keep doing the hard thing. Commit to living your life in the freedom of letting it all go and letting God fully into your life. You'll experience the greatest rewards as you continually accept the invitation to trust Him.

So here we are, faced with an opportunity: twenty-six invitations to join into deeper connection with our Father and deeper connection with our husbands. First, we get to respond to His invitation by joining Him on a journey to experience deeper connection, learning about Jesus' walk on earth. Then, we'll be challenged to practice the connection Jesus demonstrated by spending intentional time with our husbands. At *A Wife Like Me*, we've heard countless responses from wives who want more one-on-one time, more quality time, and deeper connection with their husbands. We understand what it's like to live with intention when facing the demands of children, jobs, groceries, meals, and time. We feel the tension and understand what it's like to wrestle with how to find balance.

In response, our team has prayed, planned, and poured out our hearts in these pages. We've intently looked to Christ as the Master for creating connection. We challenge you to discover, alongside us, how He wants to build connection with us and use that connection to kick-start our connection with our husbands.

The amazing women featured in these invitations are wives just like you, hoping to build connection and grow. Know that we have prayed for you, for your husband, and for your marriage.

# DEAR *Wife*,

May this invitation be a daily confirmation that God rules and reigns in your life and marriage. May your heart be overwhelmed by His goodness as you press on through these pages. May you continue to show up when it's hard, trust when you feel discouraged, and know that no act of love is ever wasted. As women walking through this experience, may we be certain that each invitation is a glorious, God-breathed step of new life and faith. May we believe in His way and surrender our own. May we not be defined by our disappointments but, instead, comforted in our connection to the King. May we be a community dedicated to growth, not perfection. May our sons and daughters see the fruit of this work and crave the same in their marriages.

*Lord, may our husbands awaken with Your love for them. May they be blessed by these invitations to ultimately know more of You. May new, fresh love blossom as hearts come alive. May our marriages glorify Your name; may we get out of the way and let You have Your way in our homes and in our hearts. May we be wives who thrive, in You and for You. Amen.*

With our deepest love,
Amanda Davison and the *A Wife Like Me* team

## How to Use This Book

At times, this might be hard. Let me rephrase that: at times, this *will* be hard. You might feel stretched or challenged. You might think an exercise that's described in an invitation doesn't make sense or is pointless. We encourage you to lean in anyway and go for it! Visit the next section any time you need to get back on track, or tell us about what is difficult in our closed Facebook group, *A Wife Like Me Gathering.*

We pray that this book won't be the end of your pursuit to build connection with your Father and your husband. We've got a great deal of content and resources to help you continue your journey at www.awifelikeme.com.

## Questions You Might Have

### What if my husband doesn't engage in the content with me?

Your husband may disengage during your attempt to connect with him, or he may choose to not engage at all. He may continue to scroll on his phone or watch television. In those moments, remember the many times God has not given up on you.

Recall the many times you have chosen something else—mindless TV watching, scrolling, or someone or something else. God always leaves the door open and never condemns you. As wives, all we can do is our own part; we are the only person we can control. Focus on keeping your heart aligned with the process, and trust God with your husband and your marriage. If your husband doesn't have an interest in your invitations to connect, respect his feelings and use the time after your reading to journal your feelings instead. Share your raw feelings with God and pray for what you desire your marriage to be. He is listening. Don't allow your husband's lack of desire to connect to cause you to disengage with God. Use this time for deeper connection with God instead, thanking Him for your continued growth in Him.

### What if my husband responds differently than I hope?

Expect this to happen. Unless you are already intentionally connecting with your husband, this time will feel new and different for your husband—so expect the unexpected. Remember that we will not gauge "success" based on the results. Instead, we will gauge success based on our own heart's willingness and acceptance of each invitation.

What a success to finish a journey of deeper connection with God! If your husband doesn't respond how you hope he will, that's a cue to back up, give him space, and journal instead. Thank your husband for hearing you, then spend time with God sharing your feelings and the prayers of your heart. He hears you.

### What if he doesn't reciprocate?

Remember that you have chosen to take part in this growth journey of connection with God and your husband. Your husband might question your motivation for reading and taking time with him and for your marriage. He might think it's pointless or weird. He might give you a mixed response, choosing to respond to you by reciprocating what you've done or said to him one day, opting not to the next. Try to remember that you are not reading this book in expectation that your husband will change or meet you where you are. You are reading this book to work on your own heart, trusting that God will use it to deepen connection with Himself and with your husband. This isn't always immediate, and it often requires trusting God's timing.

Deeper connection and growth aren't measured by immediate responses, but by an increase in heart capacity and intimacy for someone else—even if it's only in your heart for your husband. Would we love to see your husband's heart be so moved by your efforts to connect with him and sense a deeper desire for connection for His Father through your time together? Yes! We all want that and we pray this book helps to foster that outcome. But we've got to trust God with it.

### How will I know if this is working?

We'd love for you to measure whether or not this book is working by whether or not your connection with God is deepening. Try to make connecting with your Father your primary goal, and let connecting with your husband be an overflow of your connection with God. Why? Because you have control over opening your heart and spending time connecting with God. Once you've established that connection, you can put your effort toward your husband, praying that your husband engages with you and that your marriage is blessed by it. We've done our best to set your marriage up for connection, but there are some factors outside of our control. Keep showing up and focusing on your connection with God, and trust Him to increase the connection in your heart toward your husband.

### But if I'm growing in my faith to better our marriage, shouldn't he be doing the same?

This would be ideal, wouldn't it? This is God's heart and design for marriage—that together, the husband seeks to love his wife as Christ loves the church, and the woman respectfully honors her husband. And for many wives, this dual investment and intentionality is alive and active in their marriages. But for others, this isn't the case. Many wives shoulder the burden, working alone to improve their marriage or grow their faith. To these wives, we say that this is all the more reason to take part in this journey. Do not take your influence as a wife lightly. You have an opportunity to allow your own connection with God to shape how you love and seek connection with your husband and to influence your husband's heart. We pray that your husband is radically blessed by your desire to connect with God and with him, and that God would use your journey to soften your husband's heart and create a deep-seated need within him for God.

## HOW EACH INVITATION WORKS

Each invitation will start by going back in time and learning from the master of connection, Jesus himself. After discussing ways in which Jesus created connection, you will be directed to answer some reflection questions.

---

## REFLECTION QUESTIONS

Use these questions as prompts to examine your own heart. Don't rush to answer quickly. Instead, soak in them and allow God to reveal new things to you about your heart and His.

---

## CONNECT WITH THE FATHER

This time is for you to connect with God. Don't rush these moments.

---

## CONNECT WITH YOUR HUSBAND

This is your opportunity to bring what you've learned to your husband. We invite you to approach your husband and spend five minutes implementing the invitation. If you are unable to directly implement the invitation face-to-face (your husband is gone at work or otherwise not available), we've included some ideas for you, but feel free to get creative!

- Make a note to implement it once he's home.
- Journal, writing to him instead.
- Record a video and send it to your husband if he won't be home for an extended period of time.
- Text your husband to tell him what you're thinking and mention your thankfulness for him.
- Use a journal to write to God.

# Moving Toward Him

—

*While walking by the Sea of Galilee, he saw two brothers, Simon (who is called Peter) and Andrew his brother, casting a net into the sea, for they were fishermen. And he said to them, "Follow me, and I will make you fishers of men." Immediately they left their nets and followed him. And going on from there he saw two other brothers, James the son of Zebedee and John his brother, in the boat with Zebedee their father, mending their nets, and he called them. Immediately they left the boat and their father and followed him.*

**Matthew 4:18–22**

# DEAR Wife,

The music signaled the start. With the beats of the notes, my steps made forward motions toward the double wooden doors. My father and I stepped into view, stood there, and waited for our cue.

My eyes fixed on him, my groom, dapper in his black tuxedo at the end of the altar, waiting for my arrival.

In a few short moments, the pastor would begin our vows and our lives would forever be shaped around one another. I just had to make it down the aisle—one step at a time, one foot proceeding after the next. Slowly and surely I made my way to the altar. All the while, he stood perfectly still. Stable. Solid.

I didn't realize it then, but this would be the first of many times I would be the one to make the move. Walking down the aisle, walking away from my comfort zone into unfamiliar territory—this work of moving toward something new would not be a one-time event.

It was something God was calling me to do as a wife, and it began with the wedding aisle walk.

For nearly a decade of our marriage, I lived in frustration. It always seemed I was moving toward my husband, while he wasn't making the initial move toward me. I felt like I had to lead our family spiritually; I felt like I had to move toward him in reconciliation after a fight; I felt like I had to constantly be the one drawing toward him. He never seemed to be drawing toward me.

"What's the deal, Lord? Why am I the one always doing the work in this marriage? Is this how it's supposed to be? If this is the game, Lord, I'm not a fan."

Have you ever felt this way?

The thing about connection and intimacy is someone always has to initiate it. Someone has to move. If you've been the one to typically initiate growth or change, you might be weary in your attempts. Maybe you've stopped altogether. Or perhaps you're just starting to try.

Wherever you find yourself, Jesus provides us an inside look into all that is possible when we follow His example. In Matthew 4, we see Jesus' precious people, His friends, His partners—Peter, Andrew, James, and John—busy working to gather food. In the middle of their everyday routine, fishing, Jesus enters their lives and calls them to something bigger than themselves. The moment changes everything for them.

What do we see Peter, Andrew, James, and John do when Jesus calls them to be His disciples?

Immediately, they act.

Jesus stands still, and the disciples—the Church, the bride—moves.

My husband called me to himself. He asked me to be his most precious person. His friend. His partner. His bride.

---

# IT DOESN'T MATTER WHO INITIATES CONNECTION— IT JUST MATTERS THAT CONNECTION IS INITIATED

---

The Lord whispers to my soul, "I've called you to be his wife. Your job is hard. You will give up things. You are going to have to move, even when you don't feel like it or want to. But don't move away from him; keep moving toward him. Follow My instructions immediately. Listen to My call on your life and leave behind the fear, the culture, the mess, and your frustration. Trust Me. Move toward what I call you to; move toward your husband. Don't hesitate to obey Me."

It doesn't matter who initiates connection—it just matters that connection is initiated.

As you begin this book, you are given the same invitation Jesus gave to His disciples. "Follow me," Jesus said, "and I will make you fishers of men" (Matthew 4:19).

As wives, we have the opportunity to influence the trajectory of our marriage, family, and future. One step at a time. One act of obedience after the other.

Marriage is no easy calling. God will call many of us to challenging acts of obedience.

And so, the hard work of unraveling our souls begins in order for God to begin weaving new patterns in our hearts. As we learn to move toward the Lord, we also learn how to move toward our husband in holy, healthy, and more meaningful ways. As we become wives who urgently say yes to creating connection, we make room to see God move in our hearts and in our homes.

Connection doesn't happen if both parties stay stationary. Just as I had to walk down the aisle toward my husband in order to say our vows, I must constantly take action to intentionally move toward my husband in order to build connection and intimacy. It's not always easy or comfortable, but it's always worth it.

Many of the tasks we will be challenged with as wives throughout this book may feel uncomfortable, but growth doesn't happen without stretching us out of our comfort zone. All of the blessings the disciples received, all the miracles they witnessed, and all of the lives they touched and changed happened because they weren't afraid to say yes to Jesus and immediately act when He called.

Will you say yes to Jesus? To all the things He may ask? To all the uncomfortable places your soul may walk as we journey together on this road of wifehood?

You and I were brave enough to walk toward that connection when we walked down the aisle. Let's be brave and walk toward what Jesus calls us to do in our marriages.

*Father, thank You for calling me Your daughter. The assignment of being a wife to _____ is no easy task, but You have equipped me for the task. Thank You for entrusting Your precious son to me as my husband. Help me to honor him, move toward him, and lean into You as I seek to become a better wife.*

Your friend,
Natalia

_____

## REFLECTION QUESTIONS

1. How significant do you think it is that Jesus came to His disciples when they were in the middle of something and asked them to lay it aside?

   _____

   _____

   _____

   _____

   _____

2. What does the response of Jesus' disciples to immediately act say about the importance of the work they were called to do?

   _____

   _____

   _____

   _____

3. Knowing that Jesus is calling you to leave behind what you've been doing or trying in your marriage, and instead follow His lead to create connection with your husband, what feelings are you experiencing?

_____

_____

_____

_____

_____

4. Knowing you will likely experience frustration over an unequal quest for connection during this journey, how do you plan to remind yourself of the holy steps you are called to take toward your husband?

_____

_____

_____

_____

_____

Jesus modeled the importance of urgent action. The decision to follow was dependent on the disciples' response, but the outcome was not. Jesus taught and showed His people how to do the rest.

_____

## CONNECT WITH THE FATHER

If you have not yet read the introduction, please go back and read that now.

Enter into quiet time with the Lord by acknowledging the ways in which you have put off the call to act immediately to love and/or invest in His people. How have you prioritized your schedule, your plans, your comfort, or your convenience over what He has asked you to do? Come to the Lord with the realizations you've experienced and lay them at His feet. Ask God to renew in your heart the urgency of your marriage and your husband. Ask Him to instill in you a quick yes, even when it's hard. Talk to the Lord about how you can connect with your husband.

## CONNECT WITH YOUR HUSBAND

The suggestion below is a question that has worked well in my own marriage. It allows my husband the freedom to voice anything he wants to see changed in our marriage, but also allows him to affirm and encourage me as well. I, in turn, don't feel attacked when it comes as a suggestion instead of a criticism. Use it, adapt it, or expand it as you see fit for your marriage dynamic.

Go to your husband and share the following idea: "Our marriage is precious, and I know I contribute both negatively and positively. What is something in our marriage that I am doing well that you would like to see me continue doing? What is something in our marriage that I haven't done as well that you want to see me improve on or adjust?"

### Invitation 2

# Come To Me

*"Come to me, all who labor and are heavy laden, and I will give you rest. Take my yoke upon you, and learn from me, for I am gentle and lowly in heart, and you will find rest for your souls. For my yoke is easy, and my burden is light."*

**Matthew 11:28-30**

# DEAR Wife,

Back in 2000, when my husband and I started dating, we had lengthy late-night phone conversations. We paid long-distance fees adding up to hundreds of dollars for our cross-country phone calls where every minute felt special. Every hour of conversation was spent talking about the details of our day, our plans for the future, or anything else that filled the space between our phones. We loved hearing each other's voices when we weren't able to meet face-to-face.

Isn't this how it started for many of us? Long conversations that linked our hearts together?

But over the years, our conversations have become much shorter. After all, we've got children to keep alive and piles of bills to pay. We've got real-life jobs and full schedules. I can't imagine talking for hours with him now, on the phone or even in person. What once was carefree time spent enjoying each other's presence has now been boiled down to fact-sharing sessions. When we do talk to each other, we have lists:

- Please fix the shingle that is dangling off the roof.
- I need your help gathering paperwork and receipts for our taxes.
- The kids have dentist appointments Friday. Will you be able to take them or do you need me to?
- Mom is willing to watch the kids this weekend. What should we do for a date?

We love each other, but lately our marriage has revolved around the details of life rather than a real heart connection.

In those early days of our relationship, we had no agenda other than getting to know each other through long conversations and hours of being in one another's presence. While I'm glad to have a connection to my husband at all, a connection without an agenda would be even better.

How do we create margin for such connection when real life is all around us? We can look to Jesus to teach us. Jesus gives us a clear prescription for connection that fills and transforms. Jesus says that if we aren't first quieting our hearts and connecting with Him, we're missing the point. He gives our hearts rest, gentleness, humility, and light. Jesus wants to connect without any agenda at all besides love. He even goes above and beyond a surface-level love, asking His followers to cast their burdens on Him.

Doesn't that sound good in your busy, stressful life? When you feel like you're the one carrying the load? When you're trying to hold it all together and feel like you're falling apart? When you just want a place to rest and be refreshed? Wouldn't you love someone to take your burdens from you and carry them alongside you? Jesus will do that for you, dear one. As you come to Him, especially when you are weary, He will give you rest. He will also inspire you to love your husband this way. But we can't go to our husband first, expecting to receive intimate connection with him when we've bypassed the one connection that matters most. Connection with your husband starts with connection with God.

## JESUS WANTS TO CONNECT WITHOUT ANY AGENDA AT ALL BESIDES LOVE

As you make room in your day for real connection and rest with God, your heart will naturally seek to be a safe, restful place for your husband. Staying mindful that your agenda with your husband isn't only to discuss details but to truly be an oasis for him will connect his heart to yours.

Jesus wants your heartfelt long-distance phone calls. He wants the ongoing, daily details of your thoughts and desires. He wants to be with you, uninterrupted, as you share with Him how you feel and what you're carrying. He just wants you. He wants your heart. He wants you to savor the one connection that fuels your soul so you can go and foster that same kind of connection with your husband.

Your friend,
Sarah

**REFLECTION QUESTIONS**

1. When did you last spend quality time with God?

_____

_____

_____

_____

2. How might your relationship with God grow if you shared with Him like you once shared with your husband?

_____

_____

_____

_____

3. When did you last have quality conversation with your husband without an agenda or list?

_____

_____

_____

_____

_____

4. What inspires you most about Jesus' words today? How can you follow Him as your model for connection with your husband?

_____

_____

_____

_____

## CONNECT WITH THE FATHER

Take two minutes to simply close your eyes and lay your hands in front of you, palms up, in silent connection with God.

## CONNECT WITH YOUR HUSBAND

Ask your husband these questions—without an agenda—and listen well to his answers.

- When was the last time you felt at rest?
- If you could take a temporary rest from your responsibilities, which responsibility would you choose to let go?
- What is your area of greatest struggle right now?
- What one step could I take to help you bear the burden of that struggle?

Try listening to your husband's heart underlying his words the next time you connect. Let him know that you're praying for him and you're willing to help carry his burdens in practical ways.

# What We Really Need

—

On one of those days, as he was teaching, Pharisees and teachers of the law were sitting there, who had come from every village of Galilee and Judea and from Jerusalem. And the power of the Lord was with him to heal. And behold, some men were bringing on a bed a man who was paralyzed, and they were seeking to bring him in and lay him before Jesus, but finding no way to bring him in, because of the crowd, they went up on the roof and let him down with his bed through the tiles into the midst before Jesus. And when he saw their faith, he said, "Man, your sins are forgiven you." And the scribes and the Pharisees began to question, saying, "Who is this who speaks blasphemies? Who can forgive sins but God alone?" When Jesus perceived their thoughts, he answered them, "Why do you question in your hearts? Which is easier, to say, 'Your sins are forgiven you,' or to say, 'Rise and walk'? But that you may know that the Son of Man has authority on earth to forgive sins"—he said to the man who was paralyzed—"I say to you, rise, pick up your bed and go home." And immediately he rose up before them and picked up what he had been lying on and went home, glorifying God.

**Luke 5:17-25**

# DEAR Wife,

As a busy wife and mom, I seldom get time alone. Living in a house full of boys is usually loud and always busy. Last week was a particularly rough week, and my stress levels were through the roof. Everyone was busy doing their own activity, so I snuck off to get ready for bed early. Just as I was enjoying the peace and quiet of my momentary solitude, my husband came in to find out what we were eating for dinner.

Initially, I responded sweetly to him, but I quickly found myself becoming exasperated. *Seriously? After the week I had, couldn't he figure out dinner on his own or order takeout?* As my frustration escalated, I felt my sense of peace slipping away. *Must I always be the one to get dinner on the table? Can't I ever have a moment to myself?* And that is when I snapped. I blew it. Every ounce of composure I had gained immediately flew out the window, and I responded in anger to my husband. Inside, I wondered, *Why is it that I always find myself in these situations? Just when I'm able to have some alone time, it's disrupted.*

Oh, how I wish I could respond more like Jesus. Jesus lived His life on mission, willing to adjust to the needs of others. Jesus even allowed interruptions in His schedule for the sake of displaying the power of forgiveness.

In the featured passage, we learn that people gathered from Galilee, Judea, and Jerusalem to hear Jesus teach. Crowds congregated to listen to Him speak, including the prominent religious leaders of the day, the Pharisees and teachers of the law.

While Jesus was teaching, He was interrupted by some men who were carrying their paralyzed friend on a mat to seek healing. When the men couldn't reach Jesus through the crowds, they took their friend to the roof and lowered him down before Jesus. Can you imagine? In the middle of a meeting—an important dinner with coworkers or friends, or in the middle of church—when suddenly a person is lowered in from the ceiling?

After the man was lowered down in front of Jesus, He had a choice. Jesus saw that the man was paralyzed, yet He was busy teaching. The crowd hung in the balance, watching how Jesus would respond. scripture says Jesus chose to interrupt His own teaching to say to the man lowered in, "Man, your sins are forgiven you" (Luke 5:20).

Confusion set in among those watching. Why would Jesus forgive this paralyzed man? This man's friends brought him for healing, not forgiveness. What was going on? Forget that Jesus was busy and had been interrupted—why did He choose to say he *forgave* the paralyzed man? The account continues, "And the scribes and the Pharisees began to question, saying, 'Who is this who speaks blasphemies? Who can forgive sins but God alone?'" (Luke 5:21). These men were certain that Jesus could perform miracles yet were confused by His ability to also forgive sin. Yet in verse 24, He continued to astonish them when He said to the man who was paralyzed, "I say to you, rise, pick up your bed and go home."

These men disrupted Jesus' plans. They wanted Him to heal their friend physically, but Jesus knew this man needed more than that. This man didn't need physical healing as much as he needed forgiveness for his sins. The eternal gift of grace was the healing this man needed. Even though he had what seemed to be an obvious problem, Jesus knew a physical change wouldn't bring true healing.

## SOMETIMES CONNECTION ISN'T CONVENIENT

Sometimes, what presents itself as the point of conflict or division in marriage isn't what needs the most attention. Sometimes what we think our husband needs to change or what would make our heart feel better isn't actually what we need. How often do we bring our frustrations to God, wishing He would fix or change something in our lives or in our husbands? How often do we drag our "broken" husbands to Jesus, expecting Him to change their level of affection, their tendency to care about work or fantasy football, their desire to binge-watch Netflix more than spend time with us, or their lack of help around the house? When, really, what our heart needs or what our husband's heart needs most is simple, yet powerful, grace?

In the case of my dinnertime frustration, I chose to let a minor question turn into a larger argument and, in doing so, missed out on a chance to extend the grace and mercy that Jesus so often extends to me. Sure, I was annoyed that dinnertime needs were dropped into the middle of my alone time. When all we can see is what *we* need, it's easy to fixate on the sacrifice we're making, prioritizing our wants over our husband's needs. It was easy for me to blame my husband for his lack of consideration, which was the obvious need I wanted to address. But in this case, choosing to focus on my momentary frustration brought division instead of connection.

In that moment, I failed to recognize that sometimes, it's the less obvious need that requires attention in marriage. In my case, it was learning how to extend simple, unmerited favor—especially when it's undeserved. Jesus extended this to the man on the mat, just as He extends it to us, because He knew it would be far more

powerful than solving any obvious physical need. Jesus wants to provide the same power of connection in our hearts and in our marriages.

Sometimes connection isn't convenient. Sometimes it's needed as we're walking out the door or running late for a meeting. Sometimes it's needed in the silence of night when your husband is sleeping in another room. Sometimes it's needed when they are right in front of you yet feel far away. Sometimes we're the one needing the connection, while other times we know we need to extend it to our husband. Either way, Jesus made a path for connection.

After I displayed such anger toward my husband for interrupting my alone time to ask about dinner, I had to humbly go and ask for his forgiveness.

As wives, we have many opportunities to bring situations before the Lord and allow the Holy Spirit to help us discern the real need. We have everyday opportunities to see interruptions in our busy lives as holy moments appointed by God to love those around us. As wives, this means making ourselves available to our husbands, even when it is not convenient or when we would rather be doing something else. When we are able to see beyond our own needs, we're better able to see what the real need is and respond accordingly.

Your friend,
Misty

---

## REFLECTION QUESTIONS

1. How do you currently handle situations where your needs clash with your husband's needs? What would happen if you saw these differences as holy moments that offered personal growth and allowed you to demonstrate and extend grace?

_____

_____

_____

_____

_____

_____

_____

2. What are some ways you typically focus on what you see as primary needs in your marriage (communication problems, behavior patterns, preference clashes), rather than seeking God's direction on what your husband and you truly need?

_____

_____

_____

_____

_____

## CONNECT WITH THE FATHER

Like the man on the mat, Jesus never sees you as an inconvenience or intrusion. Instead, Jesus assesses the need underlying your complaint and throws you a lifeline of healing and grace, knowing what your heart truly needs. Take time now to reflect on what you've been praying for, whether it's a change in your circumstances or the desire for your husband to be or do something differently. Ask God to speak to the real need of your heart and provide you with what you're truly seeking, whether it's love, trust, peace, or healing. Soak in what God gives you.

## CONNECT WITH YOUR HUSBAND

Consider the many things you are tasked with that can feel mundane or unimportant: completing tasks around the house, parenting the kids, or supporting his personal well-being. Reflect on these things, then turn these into opportunities of thanksgiving by communicating with your husband via text, a phone call, or in person how grateful you are to do those things for the glory of God.

# Disengage with Dysfunction

And the Pharisees and Sadducees came, and to test him they asked him to show them a sign from heaven. He answered them, "When it is evening, you say, 'It will be fair weather, for the sky is red.' And in the morning, 'It will be stormy today, for the sky is red and threatening.' You know how to interpret the appearance of the sky, but you cannot interpret the signs of the times. An evil and adulterous generation seeks for a sign, but no sign will be given to it except the sign of Jonah." So he left them and departed.

**Matthew 16:1-4**

# DEAR Wife,

I didn't learn how to communicate in a healthy way in my childhood home, and neither did my husband. We both learned dysfunctional communication patterns; however, I learned better ways to communicate as an adult by working on myself in twelve-step programs and counseling. My husband, on the other hand, continued to be comfortable with unhealthy communication.

For the first twenty years of our marriage, I tried to convince him to speak differently to me. I pointed out how his communication style was wrong and tried teaching him how to communicate in a healthy way. My efforts to try and change him only made the dysfunction worse.

I remember one evening, after getting off the phone with a friend who was in a difficult marriage and sharing with her ideas on how to cope, my husband mockingly said to me, "What makes you think you can tell her what to do when you aren't perfect?"

Ouch.

Do you ever feel wrongly accused within your marriage? It's hard, and it hurts. Jesus found Himself in a similar situation, faced with accusations and questions. The Sadducees, an important social and economic group of Jews, as well as the Pharisees, a self-righteous group of Jews, approached Jesus manipulatively and mockingly by asking Him for a sign from heaven.

Regardless of their motive, Jesus refused to enter into an unproductive and unhealthy conversation. He saw their provocations as bait into dysfunctional discourse, and He refused to play their game. Jesus had already provided confirmation that He was the Son of God by performing miracles and fulfilling prophecies. If the Sadducees and Pharisees had been capable of reading them as correctly as they did the weather, they wouldn't be asking for more signs. But here they were, attempting to provoke Jesus. It was their version of "What makes you think you're so perfect?"

Jesus got to the heart of the issue by reminding them that they already had signs that they could choose to read. He also refused to add any more fuel to the fire they were attempting to start.

When my husband asked his combative question, I was forced to reconsider my own actions. Even though I knew my husband's remark was rude and unhealthy, I also knew that every time I treated him like a child by instructing him on what he should and shouldn't say made him feel less attracted to me. Every time I reacted instead of setting a healthy boundary by not engaging in dysfunctional conversation kept us stuck in a destructive cycle. Over time, those habits damaged the connection by keeping it unhealthy.

Turning to God in these moments of feeling attacked gives us discernment and strength to disengage with dysfunction and instead work to build connection. If I had reacted to my husband that evening by defending myself and criticizing his comment, the result would have been an argument that got us nowhere. By the grace of God, my response was different. Instead of pointing out how he was wrong, I got to the heart of the issue. I asked him if he was willing to commit to working on learning how to communicate in a healthy way. It was scary because it was different. It was also scary because it meant he could say no. I was investing in improving our connection in the short-term and the long-term by not provoking an argument.

We cannot be our husband's teacher and maintain a proper husband and wife relationship. There are times when we need to stop talking, stop explaining, and stop pushing, and instead disengage with dysfunctional cycles of communication.

---

## *WE CANNOT BE OUR HUSBAND'S TEACHER AND MAINTAIN A PROPER HUSBAND AND WIFE RELATIONSHIP*

---

After the Sadducees and Pharisees tested Jesus, He directed His disciples to guard themselves against their misguided teaching. In marriage, we have the same Spirit that raised Jesus from the dead living within us, and therefore hold the power to disengage with dysfunction. Tapping into God in these moments will result in deeper connection with your husband.

Your friend,
Karla

## REFLECTION QUESTIONS

1. In what ways have you tried to make your husband change by nagging and correcting him like you are his teacher or mother?

   _____

   _____

   _____

2. When you've responded to your husband with defensiveness or attacks, what has been the result?

   _____

   _____

   _____

3. Are you willing to turn to God in moments of frustration and allow Him to show you another way? If not, what is holding you back?

   _____

   _____

   _____

## CONNECT WITH THE FATHER

Take time to confess the times you've participated in dysfunctional discourse in your marriage by attempting to correct your husband in an inappropriate way. Pray to God and ask that He would help you discern when and how to disengage with dysfunction.

## CONNECT WITH YOUR HUSBAND

Play a game with yourself today. Speak only to your husband when he asks a question. Otherwise, listen. If he notices your behavior, explain that you're working on listening more.

# A Warning Shot and an Olive Branch

—

*And when Jesus saw their faith, he said to the paralytic, "Son, your sins are forgiven."*

**Mark 2:5**

# DEAR Wife,

"Are you done now?"

The question will forever ring in my ears. It was a question, a warning, and a mercy. Because I was mouthy, entitled, and angry.

It was early in our marriage, and I cannot even tell you the subject or the reason I felt hurt, but I recall his question. I remember sitting on the couch in our fixer-upper of a house and letting my husband have it. I had been boiling for a few hours and I carelessly let it all bubble over, hot, scalding, everywhere. I was mad about something he had said or done, but I had taken it up a notch with assumptions and accusations. Spitting out shameful words and foul-mouthed fury, I spent myself, not caring about the heaping mouthfuls of regret I would have to swallow later. I said hurtful things and then, finally, sat there wondering how he would respond. The silence came as quickly as a dense fog, settling over our living room.

And then my husband, with kindness in his eyes, slowly asked, "Are you done now?"

He had listened and taken bullet after bullet, and he may have sensed I would have gone for round two. I had thought about reloading. But he stepped through the fog and gave me permission to keep going, coupled with a firm and fair warning. The question said: *I see you. I hear you. But I think you should be done now. The damage here has already been too much.*

His question was enough. It humbled me. I didn't say another word. Yes, I was more than done.

As I continued to sit there, the words I had spoken echoed in my ears. Regret moved through the fog and plopped next to me on the couch. My words were untrue and meant to hurt him. And he had continued to stand there and take it. Over and over.

After a few moments, he continued, "You said some hurtful things. I am not sure how to take it all. But I don't think you meant a lot of them."

His words offered an olive branch before I even asked for forgiveness. He extended an invitation to mercy before I was worthy to receive it.

In that moment, he was Jesus to me.

In the book of Mark chapter two, we read the story about how four men brought their paralyzed friend to Jesus for healing. They went to great lengths to see their friend walk again. It's clear they weren't coming for forgiveness. But they got it anyway. Jesus prepares forgiveness even before we prepare our hearts.

The night that I expressed fury, forgiveness was ready before I was. Waiting for me until I could find the strength to give up and repent. This is the way of Jesus. He was and is always standing ready with forgiveness in His pocket. If anyone so much as looked His way with a humble heart, or showed a hint of humility like the man on the mat lowered down as a last resort, Jesus offered forgiveness. With forgiveness comes freedom from our own mess and mire. In turn, freedom fuels friendship. It fuels strong marriages.

## JESUS PREPARES FORGIVENESS EVEN BEFORE WE PREPARE OUR HEARTS

Forgiveness. Freedom. Friendship. Praise God that forgiveness fuels connection.

There have been many moments since that fateful night when I have started to go down an ugly path toward making mountains out of molehills and loading my ammunition at my husband. And then the questions play in my mind: *Could I possibly just be done now? Do I want to risk blowing up my connection with my husband with irrational bullets? Could I instead stop, check myself, and quiet my heart?*

Sometimes I am able to do that; sometimes not. But the thing about it is, even if I fire off mean-spirited words, Jesus is ready to set me free from myself and my sin again. He is armed with both a warning shot and an olive branch, willing to provide me with the opportunity to change course and do the hard work of trusting God while refusing to give into the temptation to utter harsh words, showcase emotional reactivity, or give in to the impulse to make small things huge hurdles. And my husband stole this move right from the rightful King, as these were some of Jesus' best weapons: Forgiveness. Freedom. Friendship.

Your friend,
Amy

## REFLECTION QUESTIONS

1. When was the last time you had to apologize to your spouse?

_____

_____

_____

_____

2. What does forgiveness look like in your home?

_____

_____

_____

_____

## CONNECT WITH THE FATHER

Read Luke 15. In it, Jesus tells three parables. What do those parables say about how Jesus views repentance? What does this story show us about restoration? How do these stories influence your perspective of the way in which God views us as His children?

## CONNECT WITH YOUR HUSBAND

Forgiveness and freedom bring connection to our husband. Today, harness the power of words for good by choosing to speak well of your husband, both to him and to others. Praise him for things you admire about him—like his courage, his hardworking attitude, or his fun-loving laugh.

## Invitation 6

# No Agenda

—

*Greater love has no one than this, that someone lay down his life for his friends. You are my friends if you do what I command you.*

**John 15:13-14**

# DEAR Wife,

I'm not even going to pretend to tell you I don't want a back rub from my husband if he and I are going to have sex. I most definitely *do* want a back rub if we are going to have sex. And a neck rub. And then my back scratched. And then maybe my back rubbed again.

It's so bad. It's as though there's a running commentary that starts in my brain the minute my husband needs something from me or I'm doing any task for his benefit. Unbeknownst to him, any work I do starts a running mental conversation with my husband.

- Me, folding clothes = I'm pretty sure you're making dinner tonight.
- Me, putting the dishes away = Oh, guess who's making a trip to Dairy Queen for me tonight?
- Me, giving the kids baths = You're putting them to bed because I've washed these babies clean, my friend.
- Me, feeling the front of my husband brush my backside = Watch yourself, mister, you haven't talked to me all day.

It's true. I'm downright awful to my husband inside. My selfishness meter is off the charts. I honestly don't like it. It feels yucky. Yet, it's automatic. Thoughts of needing my husband to reciprocate anything I do for him are in my head before I even see them coming. My struggle is real, friends.

Am I the only one experiencing this tension? Hopefully you understand.

Unfortunately, this selfish nature within us is, in fact, part of our makeup. After all, we are born completely in need of someone else to keep us alive. As babies, we get everything we want. We throw a fit and get a pacifier, snuggles, a toy, clean clothes, or food. *It's amazing.* We are self-centered and think the world revolves around us . . . *because it does.* I'm not even sure why we need to grow up.

And then, slowly, we have to adjust to *not* getting what we want when we want it. Toddlerhood is not for sissies (dear Jesus, together we lift up all the wives who are raising a toddler right now). We have to learn how to share and have self-restraint. We let people go in front of us. And we have to *wait for things.*

It doesn't stop there. One thing I know for certain is that our self-centered nature from birth holds real estate in our hearts even into adulthood, and marriage provides the perfect playground for selfishness to shine. Two people, with innate self-centered hearts, living together and having to work together. *All the time.* Nothing seems fair when it feels like you're giving all of yourself for the benefit of the people around you, and nothing they do in return seems to quite match your level of service.

Now that we're being honest with each other (thank you, by the way—I can tell our friendship is taking on new heights), can we agree that it feels good to be validated by our husbands when they meet our request or reciprocate doing something for us if we're doing something for them? It feels safe and secure to give and receive—even if we've nagged him into doing so.

---

# THERE IS NO GREATER LOVE THAN LOVING SOMEONE WITHOUT AN AGENDA

---

Yet what is the end result? I often find that I'm disappointed because, no matter how hard my husband tries, it's still not enough. Either I'm frustrated because I had to ask in the first place, or I feel guilty because I forced him into action when he doesn't do the same thing to me. The end result in my heart is always the same: *yuck*.

You might be asking yourself, "Why is it bad of me to want my husband to do things for me when I'm doing so much work?" While it is normal to want reciprocation from your husband, we are called to not act on this impulse. In fact, as Jesus prepared His disciples for His departure, He gave clear instruction as to how to handle this inner tension of selfishness.

Jesus didn't say, "Stop it! Quit being selfish, you self-centered humans." He didn't scold us because He knows we are self-centered and selfish. He does, however, tell us what to do about it.

In John 15:13–14, Jesus says to his friends (and, by extension, to us), "Greater love has no one than this, that someone lay down his life for his friends. You are my friends if you do what I command you."

Jesus says that there is no greater way to show your love for someone than by putting aside your self-centered thoughts and your need for reciprocation. There is no greater love than loving someone without an agenda. He doesn't deny that we are human; instead, He lets us in on what will bring the greatest connection.

I truly believe the command to love without an agenda isn't really for the people receiving it. Sure, they obviously receive the benefit of our selfless love—but the command isn't for them. It's for us. This daily practice of laying aside our desire for reciprocation from our husbands grows a greater capacity for love in our own hearts. We get to experience Jesus on a deeper level as we seek to live like Him, not like us. It is part of our intimate walk of faith, trusting He knows what He's talking about. The result is peace, abundance, and connection.

Real, genuine connection begins with a pure and selfless intent to lay aside ourselves and simply give our husbands what we've been given through Christ. After all, Jesus is the ultimate example of loving people without an agenda. He dined with His enemies, befriended prostitutes and thieves, and healed people who didn't deserve to be healed. He was and still is the lover of the unlovable. And He didn't expect anything in return.

Three things will help us lay aside our agenda when it comes to loving our husbands.

1. Jesus' idea of love and connection is countercultural. It's important for us to recognize that modeling Jesus to our husbands by caring for them sacrificially isn't a popular concept. Caring for and loving your husband even though he may not show you the same may cause your friends to think you're crazy. You may even think it's crazy. I sure did, especially because I didn't grow up having a relationship with God. The concept of loving and giving without seeking something in return is countercultural, which makes it more of a mental hurdle for us to conquer.

2. Keep your eyes on Jesus, not on your husband. By opening up your Bible and continually learning about how Jesus loved others with no strings attached, we are reminded of what the greatest love requires.

3. Remember that we usually seek reciprocation and love with an agenda when we feel the most insecure. Use those moments as opportunities to realign your heart with the One who calls you His own. When we are confident in who God says we are, we are less likely to need something in return from those around us.

*Lord Jesus, help us lay aside the selfish thoughts that so quickly enter our minds. Help us to become masters of recognizing our self-centered tendencies. Give us the strength we need to choose the greatest love we could ever pursue and to join You in walking in love without an agenda.*

Your friend,
Amanda

## REFLECTION QUESTIONS

1. When you think about the ways you typically seek reciprocity from your husband, what underlying fear is associated with the need for reciprocation? For example, if I am seeking reciprocation of my husband to "help" around the house as much as I "help," my underlying fear is that his level of service is an indication of his level of commitment (or lack thereof) to myself and our family. I am fearful he may not be invested in us and that his lack of help validates my fear: *I may not be enough.*

_____

_____

_____

_____

_____

_____

2. Part of setting aside the temptation to love with an agenda involves trusting God with what's on the other side of letting go of our need for reassurance. Are you willing to trust God with the outcome of releasing those expectations of reciprocation?

_____

_____

_____

_____

3. Reflecting on how Jesus loved, served, and healed those who were undeserving, how does His example provide the model for your own heart change? Think of specific areas where you desire to model your heart after His.

_____

_____

_____

_____

## CONNECT WITH THE FATHER

The beauty of acknowledging where we desire to see growth is that, when we give these areas to God, He is able to move and work. First, let's recognize that Jesus already loves us without an agenda. He has loved us when we most definitely did not deserve it. He already paid for our sins on the cross without holding it over our heads. He willingly chose to take on the price of our sin out of pure love so that we would have the chance to accept the gift of life through Him. This beautiful love is the greatest love ever shown. Spend time now reflecting on God's desire to connect more deeply with you by recognizing His great love, given freely for you. Then pray, asking God to create in you a heart that quickly lays down agendas tied to love. Finally, ask God how you can love your husband without an agenda.

## CONNECT WITH YOUR HUSBAND

Spend time with your husband today doing something lighthearted. Go for a walk, do a project together, or play a game. Don't worry about having an agenda; simply connect.

## Invitation 7

# Mission Makers

And when Jesus came to the place, he looked up and said to him, "Zacchaeus, hurry and come down, for I must stay at your house today." So he hurried and came down and received him joyfully. And when they saw it, they all grumbled, "He has gone in to be the guest of a man who is a sinner." And Zacchaeus stood and said to the Lord, "Behold, Lord, the half of my goods I give to the poor. And if I have defrauded anyone of anything, I restore it fourfold." And Jesus said to him, "Today salvation has come to this house, since he also is a son of Abraham. For the Son of Man came to seek and to save the lost."

**Luke 19:5-10**

# DEAR *Wife,*

I stared back at the chubby woman in the mirror and wondered how in the world her husband could think she was beautiful. Tugging at the black fuzzy sweater that clung to my middle, I tilted my face up to the ceiling, trying to keep the tears that filled my eyes from dripping down and streaking my makeup. *Isn't this the same sweater that hung loosely last year? The one that draped so beautifully?* After three outfit changes, I didn't have time to pick something else. I needed to face the music that I'd gained ten pounds since I last wore this sweater. I applied my dusty rose lipstick, popped in my favorite silver hoops, and trudged downstairs.

In a rush, my husband was downstairs sipping on the last bit of coffee. "Ready?"

I sighed, trying to hide my disappointment that he didn't tell me I looked beautiful. Immediately, the voices in my head got louder.

"You'll never be able to measure up."

"If you would lose some weight, he wouldn't be able to take his eyes off you."

"You're so fat."

"He won't find you desirable until you drop some weight."

I felt deflated, insignificant, and unattractive. I had started displacing my own negative voice with my husband's voice. It didn't matter that he hadn't actually said the words aloud. In a matter of moments, my heart was disengaged and I felt disconnected to him.

Voices are a funny thing. Whether they are our own or someone else's, we tend to let them take authority over our lives and dictate our thoughts and feelings. While sometimes they impact us positively, they can also be detrimental to our well-being and to our marriage.

There are always going to be negative voices running amuck in our daily lives. It's just the world we live in. So what do we do?

In the featured passage, we see how Jesus was passing through Jericho on His way to Jerusalem when He stopped and looked up to a tree where a man, Zacchaeus, had climbed so he could see Jesus. Zacchaeus was a corrupt and despised man who was known as a traitor. Yet when Jesus looked to Zacchaeus, He responded to him with favor and asked to spend time with Zacchaeus at his home. While this is good news for you and me—Jesus wants to spend time with sinners—it was not well received by the people in Jericho. In fact, the crowds were shocked, and the negative chatter began. Cue the gossip, cue the spreading of untruth, and cue the eye-rolling.

Yet Jesus did not let criticism deter Him from His mission. He didn't get bogged down in the grumbling of the crowd because He *knew* His mission. Satan tried to thwart His efforts, but Jesus recognized the ploy and stayed on course.

How was Jesus able to ignore the negative chatter and focus on truth? *Because He knew His calling and was confident in it.*

Jesus' mission on earth, according to Luke 19:10, was to seek and save the lost. To spend time, enjoy, and connect with those considered "less than." The lowly. The didn't-get-it-rights. The disrespectful speakers, the micromanagers, the short-fused failures. He came to fill them with His grace and set them free. He came to set *us* free. Jesus knew His mission and didn't let anything distract Him from what He was called to do. Not even the negative chatter.

Satan will also try to thwart our efforts as wives. He loves to distract and deter us. He loves when we feel disconnected from our husbands. He knows that disconnection can lead to marital conflict, which might lead to separation that could cause divorce, which then could lead to a breakdown in family, extending to the generations to follow. It's a vicious cycle. Satan wants you to forget your mission to live loved and saved so that those around you observe your experience, leading them to want that life of love for themselves.

---

# WITH JESUS IN OUR HEARTS, WE CAN LIVE OUT THE MISSION HE'S PLACED WITHIN US

---

Don't you see? Satan hates you and wants to destroy your marriage. As wives, let's fight. Let's remember our calling. Let's not let the negative chatter around us prevent us from living in harmony with our husband, whether the negative grumbling is from yourself or other people.

What negative voices in your life are impacting your connection with your husband?

Maybe your group of friends speaks negatively about their own husbands, causing you to question your marriage.

Maybe you're inundated with the world's negativity about marriage.

Maybe your family doesn't like your spouse, making it hard to stay committed.

Or maybe, like me, the voice is your own.

Whatever the reason, perhaps negativity has caused you to lose your focus when it comes to being a wife. Despite negative circumstances, let's push through and press on to the task we've been called to as wives.

It's taken years for me to stop the negative voices in my head from impacting my marriage. Even though they still come to the surface every now and then, I recognize them for what they are and I've learned how to get rid of them. I simply go to Jesus and lay all the negative voices at His feet. I ask for grace. I ask for help. By doing this, I push through and press on.

With Jesus in our hearts, we can live out the mission He's placed within us. As wives, let's resolve to let nothing stand in the way of letting God work and move through us so that connecting with God and our husbands causes the world to wonder how such beautiful intimacy exists. We are mission-makers. Let's praise God for our beautiful purpose.

Your friend,
Shannon

---

## REFLECTION QUESTIONS

1. What negative chatter is impacting your marriage?

_____

_____

_____

_____

_____

_____

2. How can you pinpoint this negative chatter and stop it at the root?

_____

_____

_____

_____

_____

_____

## CONNECT WITH THE FATHER

The same way Jesus stopped to seek out, spend time with, and build relationship with Zacchaeus is the same way Jesus seeks to spend time and build a relationship with you. Despite your mess, your past, or your struggles, Jesus wants to connect with you, right where you are. He isn't ashamed of you or embarrassed by you. He longs to spend intimate time with you. Take time now to thank God for His heart for you. And pray this prayer: *Lord, please reveal to me the negativity that I need to cut out of my life that may be causing disconnect with You and/or my husband.*

## CONNECT WITH YOUR HUSBAND

Go to your husband and tell him about the negative chatter, inside of you or in conversation with others, that is causing you to feel disconnected. Be real and vulnerable with him. If you feel led, pray with him about how to cut out the negative chatter and focus on your marriage.

# Choosing Wisely

—

*A woman from Samaria came to draw water. Jesus said to her, "Give me a drink." (For His disciples had gone away into the city to buy food.) The Samaritan woman said to him, "How is it that you, a Jew, ask for a drink from me, a woman of Samaria?" (For Jews have no dealings with Samaritans.)*

**John 4:7-9**

# DEAR *Wife,*

For years, I thought that if I spoke convincingly enough on my position about things, my husband eventually would see the logic of my way as being better than his. I, of course, was speaking from my frame of reference and perspective. What I didn't understand was that my husband was also looking at the situation from his perspective.

For instance, he was raised in a rough-and-tumble household of brothers and one little sister. I was raised with sisters. My family went out to eat a lot. His didn't. I worked during college but didn't have to pay my own way through school. He did. Those are but a few of the differences that we each brought into our marriage, and they affected how we viewed relationships and decisions. If that wasn't enough, I'm a strong-willed woman, and Keith was a trial attorney prior to becoming a state district judge. Often, we had different perspectives and we both thought we were right.

Considering all the differences each of us brings into our marriages, it's no wonder that communication can be a challenge, or that we sometimes feel a disconnect rather than a connection to our husband.

To improve our connection, we first must recognize that connection doesn't happen when we fold our arms and shut out our husband. Someone has to take the initiative and move forward to build the relationship. Jesus shows us how to do that through the words and language He used with two women in need of connection.

## Jesus Connects with the Woman at the Well

In our featured passage, Jesus overcame numerous connection challenges with the woman at the well. The passage explains the social context:

> A woman from Samaria came to draw water. Jesus said to her, "Give me a drink." (For his disciples had gone away into the city to buy food.) The Samaritan woman said to him, "How is it that you, a Jew, ask for a drink from me, a woman of Samaria?" (For Jews have no dealings with Samaritans.)

The woman at the well pointed out that their nationalities and genders posed a connection problem. Jews had nothing to do with Samaritans, and a Jewish man definitely shouldn't have spoken with a Samaritan woman. Moments into their conversation, she realized another connection problem: Jesus was a holy teacher. The woman had been married five times and was currently living with a man to whom she wasn't married. Yet in spite of their differences, Jesus found a way to connect with the woman by using language she knew and was focused on: water from the well.

This is important for us to note. Jesus didn't bring up the Ten Commandments with the woman. He didn't shame her for her sexual immorality. She was at a well with a bucket to draw water, so He talked about water. The result? He led her to understand the spiritual concept of living water from which she could drink. This living water gave her freedom from sin and was available to her through Him. Jesus shows us that in order to communicate effectively as wives, we must communicate in our husband's language.

### Jesus Connects with A Woman Caught in Adultery

In John 8:1–11, a woman caught in adultery was brought before Jesus. The scribes and Pharisees wanted to talk about the Law of Moses and the appropriate punishment for adultery, stoning the woman. Their words were filled with condemnation and death. But Jesus chose words of grace and life to speak to the woman that no doubt connected their souls on the deepest of levels. "I do not condemn you, either. Go. From now on sin no more" (John 8:11 NASB). Can you imagine how the woman's heart soared?

What do we learn from the example Jesus provided? That when our husband has done something wrong and asked our forgiveness, words showered with grace can build a soul connection and open the door to new opportunities in our marriage.

### How might we connect with our husbands using relatable language?

Understanding how Jesus related to people is a powerful tool for our marriage. When we talk to our husband using language with which he connects, it creates an opportunity for heart and mind connection with one another.

One way to connect with your husband is by considering a real-life application. If your husband is a golfer, you might use golf language. For example, if he isn't on board with getting the kids to bed at a set time, you might connect with him in the following way: "Austin, you've told me how important it is for you to go the practice range so when you play, your golf swing is natural and you play your best. Will you help me practice a bedtime routine with the kids—story, prayer, lights off—so it becomes natural for Ben and he's rested for school the next day?"

If you and your husband have trouble living within your means, you might relate the importance of financial accountability at home to financial accountability at work: "John, I know you keep a tight budget at the office. How can we apply the practice of not spending more than we can pay off each month at home like you do at work?"

---

# LANGUAGE THAT OUR HUSBANDS RELATE TO CAN HELP OVERCOME COMMUNICATION CHALLENGES AND STRENGTHEN OUR MARRIAGE

---

If your husband has been a coach or participated in a team but doesn't see the importance of paying for a reading tutor for your child, you might connect in this way: "Justin, you are such a caring coach and invest in the best equipment for the team. I believe a reading tutor for Macy would equip her in much the same way to succeed in school."

Language that our husbands relate to can help overcome communication challenges and strengthen our marriage. Jesus demonstrated how the right words can overcome communication challenges experienced due to differences in backgrounds and perspectives. By putting prayerful thought into our choice of words, we can better relate to and connect with our husbands.

Your Friend,
Debbie

## REFLECTION QUESTIONS

Take time now to reflect on how you typically approach an issue you want to discuss with your husband.

1. Has your approach built connection or created tension?

_____

_____

_____

_____

_____

_____

2. How can you communicate in a more relatable way with your husband?

_____

_____

_____

_____

_____

_____

_____

## CONNECT WITH THE FATHER

Pray this prayer:

*Heavenly Father, thank You for sending Jesus to earth to not only die for our sins but to also show us how to live. Thank You, Jesus, for loving people and connecting with them in their own unique ways. Help me love my husband as You love him. Help me communicate with him using words that he'll relate to so we can better connect and glorify You through our marriage. Amen.*

## CONNECT WITH YOUR HUSBAND

Take the next five minutes and go to your husband, wherever he is, and apply the following:

- Share with him how you want to connect rather than be divisive.
- Apologize for times you've been mad or accused him of not understanding, realizing he truly may not have understood because he was coming from a different perspective.
- Pray with your husband, asking God to help you use words that connect, rather than divide.

# Offering a Way

*"I have said these things to you, that in me you may have peace. In the world you will have tribulation. But take heart; I have overcome the world."*

**John 16:33**

# DEAR *Wife,*

What is a wife to do when her husband has a rotten day? When the weight of the world is on his shoulders and he feels overcome with stress, emotions, and burdens? Furthermore, what are we to do when he brings the rotten day home with him?

Jesus speaks directly to this when He says, "I have said these things to you, that in Me you may have peace. In the world you will have tribulation. But take heart; I have overcome the world" (John 16:33).

In their jobs, in parenting, in friendships, in marriage—even within themselves—our husbands experience difficulties. Our gift as wives who represent Christ is to sense when those difficulties arise and offer peace as an antidote.

When my husband is experiencing challenges or work stress, it closely resembles the turbulence I feel on an airplane. No one has to flash the "fasten your seatbelt" sign to warn me. Just like a plane shifting and jostling in midair, I can feel and sense that he isn't himself.

This "turbulence" brings a vast array of emotions and responses from me. Sometimes I decide to retreat. I don't want to deal with his bad day (I can barely handle my own!), so I make myself busy. *The baby needs a bath. I should probably organize my shoes again. When was the last time I cleaned the inside of the refrigerator? Actually, I really need to run to Target for a few things (after all, when is this not true?).*

Other times, I get defensive. I take it personally that he doesn't walk in the door ecstatic to see me with my messy bun and get bombarded with sticky children, half-done laundry, tabletops scattered with LEGO, Play-Doh, and homework. I get irritated, become self-focused, and miss the opportunity to see things from his perspective.

What would happen if, instead of retreating, acting defensive, or feeling frustrated in our own selfishness, we looked within and considered how Jesus wants to bring peace into the storm? What if Jesus' heart towards my husband in the midst of a challenge could be released through me? What if God wants to use me as the solution—or at the very least, a comfort?

When I sense my husband has external stress that gets directed toward me, I can offer grace.

When I see my husband acting distant during a conversation because of overwhelm from his job, I can pull him close and offer affection.

When I notice that my husband is discouraged, I can give him affirming words of encouragement, hope, and thankfulness.

But let's be real. Sometimes, I need the affirming words of encouragement, hope, and thankfulness, too.

When I think about needing help through a difficult day or situation, I can't imagine anything more comforting than being in the presence of Jesus. I picture what it would be like to be one of His disciples and experience seeing Him face-to-face as a friend.

Notice how, in John 16, Jesus tells his disciples that it is *good* for Him to go away? Wait. *How could it be good for Him to go?* What could be better than His presence?

> "Nevertheless, I tell you the truth: it is to your advantage that I go away, for if I do not go away, the Helper will not come to you. But if I go, I will send him to you." (John 16:7)

The Greek word used here to describe the Holy Spirit is *paracletos*, which means "one called alongside to help." It can be translated to many English terms, including helper, comforter, advocate, intercessor, counselor, strengthener, and standby.

Take a minute to soak that in. Who else comes to mind when you hear "called alongside to help"?

> Then the Lord God said, "It is not good that the man should be alone; I will make him a helper fit for him." (Genesis 2:18)

Helpers. Jesus sent the Helper for us all, and God makes a helper in you and me for our husbands.

---

## EVEN THROUGH DIFFICULT TIMES IN OUR HOMES AND MARRIAGES, JESUS OFFERS US A WAY FOR OUR HEARTS TO CONNECT WITH OUR HUSBANDS

---

Sweet friends, we are able to receive the Helper to equip us, so we can be a help to our husbands. Let's face it. Sometimes we're exhausted, wiped from being all the things to all the people in our homes. We've got nothing left in us. In these moments, we get to tap into the power of the Holy Spirit living within us to live out Jesus for our husbands.

Imagine what kind of an impact we could have if we, as helpmeets, partnered with the Holy Spirit—the ultimate Helper—and came alongside our husbands in the midst of their trials?

Showing up in partnership with the Holy Spirit would look very different than how I tend to show up alone. It wouldn't look like hiding or finding ways to be busy in avoidance. It wouldn't look like defensiveness, pity parties, or irritation.

We must remember that although Jesus said we will face trials in this life, we have the good news of hope and peace because He has overcome the world! Yes, reality is hard sometimes. Stress is real and our patience will be tested. Yet we can echo words of comfort to ourselves and to our husbands when we are in the midst of such challenges. We can offer peace. We can trust the Holy Spirit to do a work far beyond us by using our words, our countenance, and our love. Even through difficult times in our homes and marriages, Jesus offers us a way for our hearts to connect with our husbands. He reminds us to "take heart, for I have overcome the world." Let's delight in the confirmation that He has already won it all.

Your friend,
Elizabeth

_____

## REFLECTION QUESTIONS

1. When you sense your husband is having a hard time or is under stress, how do you tend to respond?

_____

_____

_____

_____

_____

2. How would you like to respond?

_____

_____

_____

_____

_____

3. What steps can you take to respond in a more positive way?

_____

_____

_____

_____

_____

## CONNECT WITH THE FATHER

In the same way that Jesus encouraged His disciples with the idea that He has overcome the world (despite the difficulties they faced), Jesus wants to encourage you. Jesus longs for you to lean in and enjoy the hope that His resurrection provides you. Take time now to talk to God and understand that God is in control, knowing that although you may face hard things, He has defeated the grave and overcome the world.

## CONNECT WITH YOUR HUSBAND

Take the next five minutes to approach your husband and apply the following:

Ask him if he remembers a time when he had a hard day and you responded in an unhelpful way—either by hiding/avoiding, showing anger/irritation, or having a self-pitying attitude. Confess that you realize how hurtful this behavior is in response to the situation, and ask for his forgiveness.

Use your strengths to help your husband. If you are naturally fun-loving, find a way to bring joy to a hard situation or make your husband laugh when he's had a bad day. If you're good at multitasking, offer to use your organizing strength to help him sort through a task or problem.

# Responding To His True Need

—

*And James and John, the sons of Zebedee, came up to him and said to him, "Teacher, we want you to do for us whatever we ask of you." And he said to them, "What do you want me to do for you?" And they said to him, "Grant us to sit, one at your right hand and one at your left, in your glory." Jesus said to them, "You do not know what you are asking. Are you able to drink the cup that I drink, or to be baptized with the baptism with which I am baptized?" And they said to him, "We are able." And Jesus said to them, "The cup that I drink you will drink, and with the baptism with which I am baptized, you will be baptized, but to sit at my right hand or at my left is not mine to grant, but it is for those for whom it has been prepared."*

**Mark 10:35-40**

# DEAR Wife,

My husband has worked twelve to fourteen hours a day, six to seven days a week, for our entire marriage of thirty-nine years to provide for our family. Working in our family-owned pipeline utility company places him under a tremendous amount of stress. I support him by working in the office part-time and by doing the many things for our family he isn't able to because of his hectic work schedule.

Working beside my husband has its benefits and its difficulties. On the positive side, we get to work together to build our company. On the negative side, his stress is often directed toward me. When he is under more stress than usual and it is building, I can tell. It's like a boiling teapot, building up pressure until the steam comes out and it whistles. My husband blows his lid when he is so exhausted and so beaten down that he is operating in pure survival mode. This means he is reactive—but instead of whistling he spews out anger and resentment toward me for not doing more to help him.

Often, my response has been to defend myself and get angry that he is accusing me of not helping him, because I do. This ends with both of us shutting down, walking away angry, and vowing not to do anything more for each other. Eventually, he stops feeling resentful as his stress returns to a more normal level, but by that time, we've missed out on days of enjoying each other.

No one likes to be wrongly accused or spoken to harshly. And, as women, we are particularly sensitive if our husband directs blame or unloving words toward us.

There is much to be learned from how Jesus responds to situations where He feels wrongly accused. In the featured passage, we see Jesus' disciples, James and John, come to Him with a special request: they want a privileged seat of honor next to Him in His Kingdom. It is a bold request, born out of selfishness. Jesus, recognizing that they still do not understand that He will die a painful death on the cross for their sins, responds to their request not with frustration or defensiveness but by speaking straight to their true need.

Had Jesus gotten angry at their ignorance and selfishness, He wouldn't have been able to share with them the most important benefit He had to offer. Jesus knew that James and John didn't need to sit beside Him in heaven, they needed to *get* to heaven. James and John wouldn't die on the cross beside Jesus and be buried with Him; instead, they would benefit from His sacrifice.

When we are able to restrain our natural defensive response, doors of connection are opened. When I realized this truth, I was able to respond differently to my husband's stress-fueled anger. The next time my husband was angry with me, I knew his claims weren't true. I knew that he was blinded by stress.

Instead of getting angry in return and defending myself, I looked to my husband's most important need at that moment. He was exhausted and overwhelmed. He needed more help, but in his survival mode, he was past knowing how to ask nicely. I calmly asked, "How can I help you right now?" After he told me what he needed (help on the computer), I told him I had time the next day to do more. He gave me a list.

I committed to doing everything. We walked away feeling united. Our connection wasn't broken because, like Jesus, I didn't let his ignorance of his true need sidetrack me from seeing it. Defensiveness always destroys connection.

---

# *DEFENSIVENESS*

# *ALWAYS DESTROYS*

# *CONNECTION*

---

When people are stressed, they tend to become angry, harsh, or defensive. They blame others. It is natural under those circumstances to respond angrily and defensively. Yet when we react that way, our connection is broken. If we choose instead to look beyond the poor delivery or thoughtless words our husbands may use in times of stress, we will improve our marriages. I am not suggesting you excuse verbal or emotional abuse. I am suggesting that you and I can choose to look beyond surface complaints and focus on responding to our husband's true need. That will go a long way toward building the connection our marriages crave.

Your friend,
Karla

## REFLECTION QUESTIONS

1. Why do you think Jesus bothered to ask James and John if they could drink from His cup and be baptized with His baptism?

_____

_____

_____

_____

_____

_____

2. James and John answered yes to Jesus' question. What do you think they thought they were saying yes to?

_____

_____

_____

_____

_____

_____

3. Think about how your husband treats you when he is overwhelmed and stressed. Are you willing to look beyond his words to identify his true need? How would a tempered response be a testimony of your faith?

_____

_____

_____

_____

_____

_____

## CONNECT WITH THE FATHER

Take time now to reflect on how patient God has been with you. He has heard your aches, your pleas, and your frustration. He has and will continue to stay with you and remain engaged with you, patient and listening. You don't have to prove to Him who you are. Let Him speak to your heart and trust that He will defend your name and make things right on your behalf. Dear wife, you don't have to try so hard. Allow God to work in your marriage to produce change His way.

## CONNECT WITH YOUR HUSBAND

Go to your husband and spend five minutes telling him how you desire to refrain from defensiveness and instead build connection with him. Invite him to share with you what he needs most from you that he feels he isn't receiving, and after truly listening to his response, thank him for sharing.

# The Effort

—

And on the first day of Unleavened Bread, when they sacrificed the Passover lamb, his disciples said to him, "Where will you have us go and prepare for you to eat the Passover?" And he sent two of his disciples and said to them, "Go into the city, and a man carrying a jar of water will meet you. Follow him, and wherever he enters, say to the master of the house, 'The teacher says, where is my guest room, where I may eat the Passover with my disciples?' And he will show you a large upper room furnished and ready; there prepare for us." And the disciples set out and went to the city and found it just as he had told them, and they prepared the Passover. And when it was evening, he came with the twelve. And as they were recycling at the table and eating, Jesus said, "Truly, I say to you, one of you will betray me, one who is eating with me." They began to be sorrowful and to say to him one after another, "Is it I?" He said to them, "It is one of the twelve, one who is dipping bread into the dish with me. For the Son of Man goes as it is written of him, but woe to that man by whom the Son of Man is betrayed! It would have been better for that man if he had not been born."

And as they were eating, he took bread, and after blessing it broke it and gave it to them, and said, "Take; this is my body." And he took a cup, and when he had given thanks he gave it to them, and they all drank of it. And he said to them, "This is my blood of the covenant, which is poured out for many. Truly, I say to you, I will not drink again of the fruit of the vine until that day when I drink it new in the kingdom of God." And when they had sung a hymn, they went out to the Mount of Olives.

**Mark 14:12–26**

# DEAR *Wife,*

"Just one time, I wish my husband would plan a date for us. We always enjoy evenings together, but by the time we actually get to the date, I'm exhausted. I've called the babysitter (actually, I've called several babysitters to find one that is free); I've decided what time we need to pick up the sitter; I've written all the instructions for bedtime and snacks; I've called the restaurant to make the reservation (which means I decided which restaurant we would go to); and I've reviewed every movie at our local theater to determine the one that we would like the best . . ." As this young friend shared this frustrating scene from her life, relating her weariness, her discouraged whisper, and the defeated shriek directed toward her husband, I suspect she's not alone in hearing the thought *it just isn't worth it.*

It can become easy for us, as wives, to arrive at bitterness with our husbands for their seeming lack of involvement or care regarding special time together. This frustration can easily overshadow the reason we plan anything in the first place, which is to connect. Most of the time, it's not that our husband doesn't want to connect, but we can interpret their lack of planning the details to be a lack of interest in us—when, in reality, the details just may not be the priority.

While it can be defeating to feel like the only one intentionally investing in your marriage, Jesus demonstrated that He, too, put forth the effort to connect with those closest to Him. Our featured passage offers us a peek into Jesus' intentionality in planning, preparing, and participating in a special meal with His cherished friends—those with whom He wanted to build connection and relationship.

There are five key elements we can learn from the way in which Jesus created connection through fellowship.

1. Jesus took it upon Himself to make plans and build connection. He didn't sit back in frustration and hope His friends would see the need to reach out. It didn't matter to Jesus who initiated the connection, it only mattered that the connection was built. Jesus put the plan in place; He had clearly "called ahead." His instructions were simply stated and intentionally addressed. Dinner was His idea, so He secured the location and directed the purpose for the fellowship.

2. He was flexible with His expectations. Like a Valentine's Day date, the Passover was a celebrated event. Jesus knew there would be a crowd, so His preparation included an awareness of events outside of His immediate gathering. His provision took these outside circumstances into account as He chose the perfect location for the meal. Recognizing the challenge and possible stress that might occur from people interrupting their time simply assisted in His plans, rather than frustrating them.

3. Jesus thought about His guests, their perspectives, and their needs. With His plan set in place, Jesus moved on to the arrangements for the evening. What would the conversation include? Some discussions that needed to happen could be difficult, and space would be needed for quiet dialogue. How would He focus on His disciples? What might they need from Him during this specific time? His awareness of their needs and their concerns added to His readiness and preparation for the opportunity to be together.

---

# THE CONNECTION IS WHAT MATTERS, NOT WHO CREATED THE CONNECTION

---

4. Jesus created an environment for deeper connection to be built. When they arrived, Jesus was fully present. He chose to participate in the conversation and engage purposefully with His friends. Jesus didn't rush the time or the dialogue. Verse 18 offers us the words, "as they were reclining at the table and eating . . ." Traditionally, tables were lower, and couches (of a sort) were provided for seating. The guests would lean toward the table, able to rest their head on their hand. Even the process of being seated in this way directs our understanding of the dinner as a relaxed, open atmosphere, deliberately planned for purposeful interaction. The picture illustrates slowing down, anticipating and embracing sweet fellowship.

5. Unity is possible even if our time or conversation doesn't go according to our plans. Even with the challenging conversation that took place, the evening ends on a positive note: "And when they had sung a hymn, they went out to the Mount of Olives" (Mark 14:26). Although difficult truths had been spoken during the course of their conversation, they finished in unity by singing a hymn and leaving the dinner together.

Just as Jesus valued building connection with His disciples, we too can experience the fruit of connection with our husbands as we invest in fellowship with them—even if we're the ones planning and preparing. The connection is what matters, not who created the connection. Quality time and connection with your husband is key to a fulfilling marriage.

As you plan, prepare, and participate in fellowship with your husband, deeper connection will follow your time together.

Your friend,
Susan

---

## REFLECTION QUESTIONS

1. Have you become bitter or resentful because you have put more effort into planning time together as a couple?

_____

_____

_____

_____

_____

2. How might your marriage look different, or how might you grow as a couple, if you dove in and set your marriage up for success for more time spent together?

_____

_____

_____

_____

_____

---

## CONNECT WITH THE FATHER

Focusing on your own life, ask God to reveal any areas of bitterness you may feel toward your husband for a lack of effort. Pray, telling God how it makes you feel, and then releasing your concerns to God. Ask Him to set your mind on the goal of connecting with your husband, regardless of who has created the connection. Talk to God about how you'd like Him to breathe new life into your desire to plan or prepare one-on-one time with your husband.

## CONNECT WITH YOUR HUSBAND

Just as Jesus planned a meal for His disciples, plan a meal for your husband. If you have children, feed them earlier in the evening. Once they're in bed, enjoy a special meal together—just the two of you.

# With Hands

—

*And when Jesus entered Peter's house, he saw his mother-in-law lying sick with a fever. He touched her hand, and the fever left her, and she rose and began to serve him.*

**Matthew 8:14–15**

—

*And as Jesus passed on from there, two blind men followed him, crying aloud, "Have mercy on us, Son of David." When he entered the house, the blind men came to him, and Jesus said to them, "Do you believe that I am able to do this? They said to him, "Yes, Lord." Then he touched their eyes, saying, "According to your faith be it done to you." And their eyes were opened. And Jesus sternly warned them, "See that no one knows about it."*

**Matthew 9:27–30**

# DEAR Wife,

When we were dating, I couldn't keep my hands off him. I wanted to touch him all the time, and I couldn't wait to get to touch him like married people do, if you catch my drift.

But after our honeymoon, the enemy swooped right in and took away my sense of feeling. I had no desire to touch my husband, and when he tried to touch me, I pulled away. It wasn't because I didn't love him; I just wasn't excited to be intimate with him like I had been prior to marriage.

Every once in a while, I would get the urge to exercise the physical touch portion of the five love languages and it would take my husband by surprise. Bless his heart, it was just enough to taunt him, because weeks would pass before the next "touchy" spell.

I began to realize how important my touch was to him—and it didn't have to be sexual. Touching his hand, rubbing his shoulders, or even hugging him made him feel loved. I had underestimated the power of my touch before taking it away.

So often, the first thing to get put on the back burner when we're trying to keep up with the demands of life is intimate time with our husbands. The list of reasons we fail to pause and intentionally engage in physical touch (sexual or nonsexual) are many. We've been working all day, or we're exhausted from errands, cleaning, appointments, meal-planning and everything in between. Oftentimes, the last thing we want is to touch or be touched by our husbands.

I'm busy touching lots of lives with my day job while I neglect touching the life of the man that has been given to me by God. Can you relate?

Yet Jesus modeled just how vital touch can be as He healed people throughout scripture by physically, emotionally, and spiritually touching them. Here's an example: "And when Jesus entered Peter's house, he saw his mother-in-law lying sick with a fever. He touched her hand, and the fever left her, and she rose and began to serve him" (Matthew 8:14–15). Jesus pulled the fever out of a sick woman through touch. Think about the disease of loneliness you can pull out of your husband just by touching him and reminding him you are there as his helpmate and his partner in this life.

Jesus' touch brought healing power to brokenness. Jesus is all-powerful and could have healed without touch. But He chose to use the power of touch to connect, to heal, and to restore. As people, we are created for intimate connection, where the act of sexual pleasure and oneness brings glory and honor to the union of marriage and to God. There is great power and great connection through touch.

Yet all too often, as Christians—especially as Christian married couples—we aren't always great advertisements for sexual or nonsexual enjoyment and fulfillment. Growing up in a church and home where sex was rarely discussed, the message I received about sex was how I should avoid it. It's a common theme amongst my friends, where many of us have been taught that "sex is bad" rather than "sex is holy." Because of this, I've found that Christians often limit or downplay the essential ingredient to a healthy, strong marriage, which is intimate connection through physical touch and sexual intimacy. We have somehow become convinced that intimate connection should come before physical intimacy, and we've found it acceptable to withhold the very act for which we were created.

If you know you need to connect with your husband by touching his hand and/or initiating sex, then resolve to put down your phone, stop cleaning the kitchen, turn Netflix off for the night, and go get your man.

# *YOU BUILD CONNECTION THROUGH TOUCH*

My husband and I have been married for a year and a half, and I am just now learning how to be selfless enough to drop all the "important" things I'm doing to sit with my husband and hold his hand. I still fail far too often, but Jesus is teaching me that my husband is more important than most of the things I'm spending my quality time on.

Through touch, Jesus brought life into physical bodies and drew hearts to the Father. The same power of touch is available to you and your husband. You build connection through touch.

If your husband is the one who hasn't wanted to be touched lately, talk to him. Let him know how deeply you want to be with him physically and pray with him about reviving your physical relationship. We have to make physical intimacy with our husbands a priority, even on the hardest days. Even when the laundry multiplied overnight. Even when work exhausted us. Even when our friends want to go grab dinner. The healing power of Jesus lives in you and gives you the permission and prompting to bring new life and connection into your marriage through touch. Begin saving your marriage with the touch of your hands.

*God, we know You created physical touch to have healing power. Hugs show love, high-fives change moods, and kisses release endorphins. Help us to use this gift You've given us to show our spouse how much they mean to us. Give us the desire to be intimate with our husbands even when we are physically exhausted. Remind us it is an honor, not a chore, to make love to our husbands. You created sex, and we want to do it the way You designed it. Show us new ways to touch the life of our husband, and let our greatest ministry be at home. Amen.*

Your friend,
Kaitlin

## REFLECTION QUESTIONS

1. How significant do you think it is that Jesus chose to touch those in need?

_____

_____

_____

2. What does Jesus' touch provide?

_____

_____

_____

3. Reflect on how you've spent time over the past month touching your husband, sexually and nonsexually. How is the Lord prompting your heart to make changes?

_____

_____

_____

4. Knowing you were created for sexual intimacy with your husband, and that sexual intimacy is a basic human need, how might sexual intimacy be the doorway to improvement in other areas of your marriage?

_____

_____

_____

_____

_____

## CONNECT WITH THE FATHER

Spend time now in conversation with God about your physical desires. Ask God to purify your heart from any past sexual sin, fear, or hesitancy. Pray for courage to create physical closeness and connection with your husband.

## CONNECT WITH YOUR HUSBAND

Jesus modeled the power of touch, which you have access to with your husband. Go to your husband and communicate the following, adapting it to how you feel comfortable: "I want to serve you through touch. What sort of touch would you like that to be?" Ideas include a back rub, a hug, cuddling while you watch a movie, a passionate kiss, or something else.

# When We Forgive Much

—

*And he said to her, "Your sins are forgiven." Then those who were at the table with him began to say among themselves, "Who is this, who even forgives sins?" And he said to the woman, "Your faith has saved you; go in peace."*

**Luke 7:48–50**

# DEAR *Wife*,

The big, fluffy chair surrounded me and begged me to relax as my feet soaked in the small tub of warm water. Even though the room was filled with the peace and presence of God, I couldn't seem to let go of the feelings of shame that seemed to engulf me. Tears streamed down my cheeks as my husband knelt low, tested the water's temperature, and began to wash my dirty feet. It wasn't something I felt comfortable with because I felt unworthy. Full of shame. Dirty. But there we were, following through with what our marriage counselor advised could be very healing for both of us.

And healing it was.

Just six months earlier, I had betrayed my husband in the worst possible way. Now, there he was, taking a place of humility by serving me in the most tender way. I instantly felt Jesus' forgiveness and grace mirrored through my husband in one of the most beautiful moments we've shared together as a married couple.

In marriage, feeling hurt is inevitable. Maybe you've been hurt by apathy or unappreciation. Maybe you've been hurt by infidelity. Maybe you've been hurt by lies and secrets.

Whatever it is, we're all faced with feeling hurt in marriage. And we're all faced with what we'll do *with* our feelings of hurt. When we feel hurt, there is an opportunity for connection to either be built or lost based on our response. When you learn to extend forgiveness, it sparks a connection that can change the course of your marriage.

In Luke 7, we read about a woman who was broken, desperate, and lost in the depths of sin. She sought Jesus, wanting so badly for Him to release what she herself could not. She came to Him crying, so much so that her tears began to fall down on to Jesus' feet. She loosened her hair (which was frowned upon) and proceeded to wipe and dry Jesus' feet with her hair, as she had nothing else to use. Those watching rolled their eyes over the actions of the "sinner" who was touching Jesus. Jesus could have ignored the grumbling crowd, but instead He chose to acknowledge them after first addressing the woman.

> And he said to her, "Your sins are forgiven." Then those who were at the table with him began to say among themselves, "Who is this, who even forgives sins?" And he said to the woman, "Your faith has saved you; go in peace." (Luke 7:48–50)

She found grace and forgiveness at the feet of Jesus.

My dear sister, Jesus forgives much. This woman came to Jesus broken and beyond repair and left completely forgiven, free, and restored. What we learn from this grace-filled story is that because we have been forgiven much, we must forgive others. Not only that, we must forgive to an even greater degree.

---

## AS HARD AS IT IS SOMETIMES, EXTENDING JESUS CHRIST'S FORGIVENESS TO OUR HUSBANDS IS THE MOST CHRISTLIKE GIFT WE CAN OFFER, AS HE TOO IS ABLE TO EXPERIENCE THE RESTORATION AND FREEDOM THAT COMES FROM FORGIVENESS

---

Have you experienced such forgiveness by bringing your own mess to the Lord? Have you allowed the cross to bear your sins and made the choice to walk in the freedom for which Christ died for you to live? If not, Christ offers this to you today. He wants to give it to you.

As hard as it is sometimes, extending Jesus Christ's forgiveness to our husbands is the most Christlike gift we can offer, as he too is able to experience the restoration and freedom that comes from forgiveness.

Maybe you are afraid to forgive your husband. Maybe you fear that, by forgiving, you are in some way saying that what he did was okay or that his offense isn't that serious. Maybe you're afraid that if you forgive he'll never receive justice. This is understandable, especially from a human perspective. But we must remember that forgiveness is a matter of faith. We can't do it on our own. We must ask Jesus for help. When we come to Him, just as the sinful woman did, God will do what is right.

When we place all of our fears into God's hands, we are free to move past the offense and see our husband through the Father's eyes. Forgiveness and love break through, and restoration happens. A marriage that was previously broken and torn is made free and whole—because of Christlike forgiveness.

The sinful woman who washed Jesus' feet desired forgiveness—but the act of washing feet isn't only for the sinner, it's for those who have been hurt by others. It's illustrated again when Jesus washes the feet of His disciples, showing them that even though they would wrong Him, He loved them and forgave them in advance.

It's been several years since the beautiful foot-washing experience with my husband. It's a memory that is etched in my heart and soul. As hard as it was to accept the love and forgiveness from Jesus and from my husband, it was a prerequisite to extending that same love and forgiveness back to him.

Although I wish I would have made better choices early on in my marriage, I am so grateful for the journey we've traveled. Because of grace, our marriage today is truly a miracle. And because of forgiveness—both received and given— we have a restored and revived marriage that has stood the test of time.

Christ built ultimate connection with us and the Father through His sacrifice on the cross and the forgiveness of our sins. Connection with your husband is built when you extend this same forgiveness to your husband. The greatest marriages choose to forgive, because it produces an equally satisfying and authentic relationship that echoes the freedom and forgiveness that Christ offers us.

Your friend,
Shannon

## REFLECTION QUESTIONS

1. Do you believe that forgiveness can change your marriage?

_____

_____

_____

2. Are you harboring past offenses? How is that impacting your marriage?

_____

_____

_____

3. Have you experienced barriers in your quest for forgiveness? What fears or concerns have held you back?

_____

_____

_____

4. Does the story of Jesus forgiving the sinful woman help you see that forgiving your husband will bring peace and connection? Why or why not?

_____

_____

_____

## CONNECT WITH THE FATHER

Spend time now reflecting on the forgiveness that Christ has offered you. Talk to God and thank Him for the sacrifice that was made because of His great love for you. Soak in the forgiveness He extends to you.

## CONNECT WITH YOUR HUSBAND

Take that same mercy, grace, and love, and extend it to your husband.

- Communicate past hurts and areas of unforgiveness to your husband.
- Explain that because you care more about growing your connection with him, you've released past pain God and chosen to fully forgive him.
- If you feel the Lord prompting you, take time in the coming days to wash the feet of your husband.

# A Choice in The Response

—

*And a man was there with a withered hand. And they asked him, "Is it lawful to heal on the Sabbath?"—so that they might accuse him."*

**Matthew 12:10**

# DEAR Wife,

Fuming and about to explode, I tried to keep my mouth shut, instead frowning in his direction. Unfortunately, he didn't get the hint. We were on a date at one of our favorite restaurants, for goodness' sake. What was wrong with wanting to enjoy each other's company, free of distractions?

He and I had passionately agreed to protect date nights. Spending vital time together, just the two of us, helped us connect and get away from life's demands. This precious alone time has breathed life into our marriage. And we were both on the same page about the necessity of being distraction-free while alone together.

So there we sat, me expecting my husband's undivided attention, while my husband sat on his phone. Finally, the words broke loose. I criticized him about talking to others through a screen more than face-to-face with me. And on a *date*, of all things.

"I'm right here in front of you—do you see me?" I spewed with a death glare.

My husband attempted to explain the necessary reason for looking at his phone, as he was expecting an important call or text from a staff member at the church where he serves as lead pastor. I wasn't interested. I wanted my husband to know that being on his phone while on a date with me was wrong and hurtful. Never mind the fact that I had just been on my phone checking in on our children. Didn't he remember what we agreed on? Yet he dared to correct me.

In moments like these, where we question each other's character, the potential for destructive communication and dynamic emotions is high. The truth is, I occasionally check my phone if I'm concerned one of the kids might call. But I went on to defend my point and myself, acting as my own legal counsel. I even justified my choice of words and angry tone. Yet the damage was done. We exchanged harsh words across the table and, by the time our food arrived, we were both upset. I lost my appetite and ended up in the restroom in tears.

Oh, how marriage offers an abundance of hard moments. Moments where we want to be right and want our husband to admit he is wrong.

Similar to my date night fiasco, the story behind our featured passage shows Jesus refusing to become defensive when unjustly accused (Matthew 12:9–15). As Jesus entered the synagogue, He turned his full attention and compassionate nature to a man with a withered hand. Hoping to trap Christ with an unlawful act on the Sabbath, a day set aside for rest, the Pharisees posed a question to Him: "Is it lawful to heal on the Sabbath?" Jesus responded in a way that let them know He valued people over rules. But the Pharisees weren't pleased with His response,

and the character attack began. Verse 14 states that "the Pharisees went out and plotted how they might kill Jesus."

The Pharisees criticized Jesus for "being on His phone." Okay, not really. But they were criticizing Jesus for something one of the ten commandments said not to do (work on the Sabbath). The Pharisees thought if Jesus were truly the Son of God, He would follow all ten commandments, which meant no work and no healing on the Sabbath. Instead, Jesus appeared to be going back on His word, just like your husband appears to do when he's on phone after agreeing not to look at it.

## AS WIVES, WE HOLD THE POWER TO RESPOND AS JESUS ONCE DID

In that moment, Jesus had center stage to let the Pharisees know they were wrong. Jesus could've dropped the proverbial mic by putting the Pharisees in their place and counterattacking. But instead, because Jesus valued relationship and connection over the need to prove Himself, verse 15 notes how Jesus chose to withdraw from that encounter even as "many followed him, and he healed them all."

He didn't engage in a verbal attack. He didn't give in to the temptation to defend. Instead, He withdrew. He offered grace instead of the gratification proving them wrong would have provided. When we belong to Jesus, He defends us. And Christ defends marriage with the best interests of both husband and wife in mind.

Sure, too much phone time takes away from intimate conversation and personal connection with our spouse. Yet it is sometimes necessary to approach the situation with grace and understanding. When we handle the situation the way I approached it—with anger and defensiveness—those responses fuel defensiveness and disconnection.

Jesus didn't need to defend Himself. And through His example, He illustrated how human compassion and grace fuel connection.

As wives, we hold the power to respond as Jesus once did. We can either choose to be angry and defend our point or offer grace to our husband. He might make a false assumption about us, may say something out of line with our character, or defensively share what we're doing wrong after we've opened up to him about our frustration. Regardless of his response, if we choose to speak the truth—in love, not from a place of emotion and disrespect—I believe it will change our heart, the heart of our husband, and our marriage.

Choosing connection with your husband over the desire to be right will look different depending on the situation. Sometimes conversations need to take place and sometimes they don't. Unless we connect with the Father, we won't be able to determine which ones are necessary. Remember that Jesus didn't feel the need to prove Himself, to justify, or to point out how wrong the Pharisees were in conversation. Instead, He knew that the Father understood His heart. His heavenly connection with the Father drove Jesus' desire to, in turn, choose to connect with people.

Your friend,
Karen F.

## REFLECTION QUESTIONS

1. There are many obvious occasions where we communicate with respect, love, and truth. Yet because we're human, there are also many instances where we give in to responding and communicating in disrespectful, unloving ways that aren't helpful. In what ways can you model the compassion and grace of Jesus to your husband instead of giving in to the need to make your point and defend it?

_____

_____

_____

_____

_____

2. How can you relay to your husband, in a loving manner, your wish for him to connect with you in face-to-face conversation and personal communication? How can you trust God in guiding your husband's heart?

_____

_____

_____

_____

_____

3. Are you willing to let Jesus defend your cause, your husband, and your marriage? Can you see it as His job and not yours?

_____

_____

_____

_____

_____

Jesus modeled how connection is possible without the need to defend or make right what others think is wrong. As difficult as it must have been, Jesus allowed the people to hold false beliefs about Him rather than engaging in damaging conversation.

## CONNECT WITH THE FATHER

Jesus wants to connect with you. Part of this connection is giving Him full control of your desire to clarify and be *right*. Take time now to let God search your heart in considering how you might sometimes engage in disagreement rather than valuing connection. Pray and ask God to give you a heart that is humble, trusting the Lord will defend your name and work out false accusations or assumptions. Ask God to give you the strength to withhold from engaging in unhelpful discussions with your husband.

## CONNECT WITH YOUR HUSBAND

Brainstorm three things you love about your husband—how hard he works, what a good dad he is, how he brings you coffee in the morning, etc.—and communicate those to him.

# Right in Front of Us

—

*And they came to Jericho. And as he was leaving Jericho with his disciples and a great crowd, Bartimaeus, a blind beggar, the son of Timaeus, was sitting by the roadside. And when he heard that it was Jesus of Nazareth, he began to cry out and say, "Jesus, Son of David, have mercy on me!" And many rebuked him, telling him to be silent. But he cried out all the more, "Son of David, have mercy on me!" And Jesus stopped and said, "Call him." And they called the blind man, saying to him, "Take heart. Get up; he is calling you." And throwing off his cloak, he sprang up and came to Jesus. And Jesus said to him, "What do you want me to do for you?" And the blind man said to him, "Rabbi, let me recover my sight." And Jesus said to him, "Go your way: Your faith has made you well." And immediately he recovered his sight and followed him on the way.*

**Mark 10:46–52**

# DEAR *Wife,*

The phone buzzed on the edge of the coffee table as I walked over to answer it. My Bible study group had ended, and I was anxious to work on some projects now that all the girls had been ushered out the front door.

As I reached for my phone, I realized my husband was calling. I answered and heard his voice, tense from workday stress, as he asked me about my small group and my plans for the afternoon.

"I planned to work on some projects I wanted to tackle. Why?" I asked.

"Oh, it's just been a long day already and I was wondering if you wanted to go to lunch with me."

*Ugh.* This wasn't part of the plan. It was not a great time. The house was empty and quiet, and I had so much work to get done. This was not a convenient invitation. Couldn't he just grab a burger and eat alone?

"If you can't do it, I understand," he offered as the silence lingered.

"No—it's okay. I can finish projects tomorrow. I would love to meet you. Where should we meet?" I replied.

Oh, the countless times my response has looked different than this particular day. There have been many times I've turned down opportunities to choose my marriage or my husband—more often than I'd like to admit. Scurrying to finish the dishes instead of reciprocating my husband's touch of affection. Dismissing invitations to engage in playful interaction because I'm too focused on my to-do list. Turning down intimacy because my book was more interesting. The list of times I've chosen my own agenda or plan over investing in my husband are countless.

I've said "no" too many times to the needs of my husband. I've brushed off his requests as annoyances instead of invitations to enter into a space of intimacy and connection with him. My day is already so full that my capacity to care for my husband has felt like too much. After all, there are so many plates I'm spinning: the kids' schedules. Their homework. Meal planning. Leading a business and ministry. Helping my husband's business. Keeping the house in order. Volunteering with our women's ministry at church. All while trying to care for myself. Too many times, I have felt exhausted and thought the only option was to hope my husband would simply understand. I hoped he would instinctively know that there were so many other things that were important, and that someday, it would get better.

But Jesus has taught me to live differently. His example has helped me to live a more balanced life. When I look at the story of Jesus in Mark 10, I see Him doing many things. He was getting ready for the holiday of Passover, a time when God freed the children of Israel from slavery in Egypt, as well as preparing for His final days on earth before His crucifixion. He had a lot of work to do. Yet, as He and His disciples were walking through the town of Jericho on their way to do important work, they were stopped by a man calling out. It was a man who needed something from Jesus—healing only He could provide.

## LET'S DO WHATEVER IT TAKES TO STEP INTO THE CALLING OF BUILDING DEEPER CONNECTION IN THE MINISTRY RIGHT IN FRONT OF US: OUR MARRIAGE

Jesus could have kept going. He could have said, "Sorry, I can't. I have to get to Jerusalem; I'm not scheduled to stop here today. I don't have time, and I have important work to do in Jerusalem. Don't you know My mission? It's a big deal. It's salvation." Instead, we see Jesus stop. He calls forth this blind man and heals him. Yes, Jesus had important work to do, and a lot on His proverbial plate. But in the midst of all of the plates He had spinning, Jesus wasn't overextended. He didn't burden His heart or His schedule to the point of neglecting the real priority: people. Jesus didn't see this man as annoying or frustrating; instead, He saw the encounter as an invitation to ministry.

It's taken many years for my heart to be softened enough to hear the Holy Spirit whisper to me when my schedule neglects a ministry God has entrusted to me— my marriage and family. Instead of choosing to live an unbalanced life, giving my best energy to things outside of my marriage, I can step into the space God wants me to fill in the important ministry of my marriage.

As women, our days are full. Coupled with our natural tendency to believe everything we do is equally important, the probability of us seeing the needs of our husbands as inconvenient is high. Whether at work, in our homes, or in our marriages, we will be faced with many moments that highlight the tension between an unbalanced rhythm of life and an intentional, unforced pace of living that reflects marriage as a priority. Let's do whatever it takes to step into the calling of building deeper connection in the ministry right in front of us: our marriage.

Your friend,
Natalia

_____

## REFLECTION QUESTIONS

1. Knowing that Jesus was on His way to do important work, yet still was willing to stop and help the blind man, how can you rethink your own work and schedule in order to be available to your husband?

_____

_____

_____

_____

_____

2. Is there margin in your day or schedule to answer the invitation to do ministry in your marriage when God calls?

_____

_____

_____

_____

_____

3. Is your heart tender toward the needs your husband has in your marriage, or are you quick to dismiss him and move on?

_____

_____

_____

_____

_____

4. Do you create space in your marriage to intentionally pray for God to allow interruptions to your life that will draw your husband toward the Lord?

_____

_____

_____

_____

_____

## CONNECT WITH THE FATHER

Take time now to reflect on whether you've been viewing your marriage as your God-given ministry. Confess any areas of selfishness or lack of care and concern for your husband. Admit where you've been more concerned with your own needs than the heart of your husband. Sit in the grace God pours out to you as you give these things to Him.

## CONNECT WITH YOUR HUSBAND

Take time now to plan how you will adjust your schedule this week in a way that shows your husband that you consider your care and love for him as your main ministry. Do you need to call a sitter, skip an exercise class, and take him to dinner? Do you need to delete Facebook or Instagram off your phone? Do you need to take a day off work to take care of things at home? Brainstorm and then make your plan.

# Exposed and Free

—

*Now when Jesus returned, the crowd welcomed him, for they were all waiting for him. And there came a man named Jairus, who was a ruler of the synagogue. And falling at Jesus' feet, he implored him to come to his house, for he had an only daughter, about twelve years of age, and she was dying. As Jesus went, the people pressed around him. And there was a woman who had had a discharge of blood for twelve years, and though she had spent all her living on physicians, she could not be healed by anyone. She came up behind him and touched the fringe of his garment, and immediately her discharge of blood ceased. And Jesus said, "Who was it that touched me?" When all denied it, Peter said, "Master, the crowds surround you and are pressing in on you!" But Jesus said, "Someone touched me, for I perceive that power has gone out from me." And when the woman saw that she was not hidden, she came trembling, and falling down before him declared in the presence of all the people why she had touched him, and how she had been immediately healed. And he said to her, "Daughter, your faith has made you well; go in peace."*

**Luke 8:40-48**

# DEAR Wife,

It was a very special day for my husband. In fact, it was special for our entire family. As an executive pastor, Tim's main responsibility was managing all the behind-the-scenes operations of the church. As a business major, he loved that. On this special day, however, he was preaching in the Sunday service for the very first time.

I'm not sure who was more nervous, him or me. That morning, I woke up extra early so I could send him off with a special breakfast before he left at 7:30. Our oldest daughter was barely two, and our second was a newborn. Waking up early was a huge sacrifice.

Breakfast turned into a large spread: bacon, homemade pancakes, and scrambled eggs. Between nursing the baby, taking care of our toddler, cooking a large meal, getting the girls dressed, and getting myself ready, I was already exhausted. It wasn't even 7 a.m. and I was sweating and overwhelmed. However, I was determined to make this day special.

As part of my plan to create the perfect day, I convinced myself I had time to clean the entire kitchen before I left for church with the girls. I didn't want my husband coming home to a disaster of a kitchen on his special day. My perfect plans suddenly took a wrong turn. As I was quickly cleaning, I spilled bacon grease all over the floor and all over myself. Ironically, the only way to clean bacon grease from a hardwood floor is to pour white flour all over the mess and let it soak (thanks, Google). I poured white flour all over the floor and surrendered to the fact I would have to leave it there until we got home.

Still determined to make the day perfect, I changed my clothes, which were also covered in bacon grease. In that moment, I realized all my clean pants were in the washing machine. *Damp.* I'm not sure if you've ever put on damp jeans. I can tell you from experience, it's not easy. I quickly changed my shirt and hurried to church with the girls.

The morning was not going as planned, but I was still determined to make it perfect. As I unloaded the kids from the car, I caught a glimpse of my belly button through my shirt. I was in such a rush that I never looked at myself in the mirror. My shirt was see-through.

I sat in the front row, feeling exposed and vulnerable. *How did I get here?* I wondered, even as I held back tears of stress, overwhelm, exhaustion, and embarrassment. The tears weren't just about that day. For the first time, my public exposure brought clarity to a truth I had tried to hide, even from myself.

I would do anything I could to appear perfect, even if that caused me to slowly wither inside.

I'm not the only woman who has ever struggled in feeling exposed. We see a similar picture in Luke 8, when Jesus is on His way to the synagogue to help the synagogue ruler's dying daughter. As Jesus made His way to see this young girl, He was surrounded by a large crowd. Within the large crowd was a woman who had been sick for twelve years and was in need of healing. She was done trying to hold everything together and desperately sought relief from her pain. She knew the only way to experience healing and freedom was to seek Jesus. She may have worried about the crowds of people, the potential for public judgment and shame. And yet, she took the risk.

## THE FREEDOM THAT RESULTS FROM CONNECTION WITH GOD IS WHERE CONNECTION WITH YOUR HUSBAND BEGINS

Reaching out, she touched the hem of His garment. When she did, Jesus immediately stopped what He was doing to ask who had touched Him. Ignoring the denial of the crowd and Peter's protest that Jesus was in a crowd and could have been touched by anyone, Jesus persisted. He asked again, and it's at that point that the woman stepped forward, trembling.

It's the courageousness of this moment that resonates on a day like my see-through-shirt Sunday. You see, even though the woman was fearful, she came out of hiding. She decided she was ready to expose her weakness and what held her back from freedom. It was worth the risk.

In that moment, she had to have faith to believe that Jesus offered what she needed. After so many years of being sick, she must have feared His reaction, perhaps even His rejection. And yet, when she fell down before Jesus, He responded with grace and mercy: "Daughter, your faith has made you well; go in peace" (Luke 8:48). In that moment, the woman was no longer hidden, but healed. She brought her hurt to Jesus and experienced the freedom she longed for.

Unlike this woman, my see-through exposure wasn't intentional, but the result was the same. The reality was that I was unable to pull off the perfect life I had tried so hard to maintain, and that realization forced me to finally expose my own overwhelm and exhaustion. In order to receive the freedom and release we desire, we must come clean with what we've been holding on to so tightly.

Admitting our need isn't easy. When the laundry is piling up, the house is a disaster, and my to-do list seems never-ending, I find myself once again thinking that I can manage on my own. That I can hold it all together and present a perfect picture of the life I so badly long to have. If you're anything like me, our tendency in these situations is to keep relying on our own strength, just like the woman who presented herself to Jesus had for twelve years. Yet trying to control our marriage and family by doing it all within our own power only serves to keep us exhausted and stressed.

Are you currently overwhelmed? Do you ever feel like a fraud? Do you desire the freedom and healing that's on the other side of exposure? Jesus wants us to come to Him with our weary, burdened hearts. When we confess our need for Him, He reacts with perfect love. There's no need to hide our mess from Him. He longs to connect with us and give us the true healing we've been seeking, if we're courageous enough to admit we need it. The freedom that results from connection with God is where connection with your husband begins.

Your friend,
Kristin

_____

## REFLECTION QUESTIONS

1. Do you ever fear exposure in your own life? What are the things you try to hide, even from yourself?

_____

_____

_____

2. Is anything holding you back from bringing the things that hinder you to Christ?

_____

_____

_____

_____

_____

3. How would exposing your true self to Jesus change your life and your marriage?

_____

_____

_____

## CONNECT WITH THE FATHER

Think of what it would be like to be the woman in this story. She had been sick for twelve years, plagued with shame and disease. She may even have been marked with the label of an outcast. Yet Jesus welcomed her, exactly as she was. In the same way, your Father turns to you, exactly where you are today. He makes time for you, He sees you, and He welcomes you. He is never inconvenienced by you. He wants to restore your peace and give you rest and freedom. How does this feel? Take time now to come clean with any way you've been striving for perfectionism, relying on your own strength, or believing you can manage on your own. Embrace God's favor and presence.

## CONNECT WITH YOUR HUSBAND

Make a list of all of your responsibilities. Next to those responsibilities, mark any you can either delegate or remove. After you're done, involve your husband in a discussion of your findings, and see if he wants to make a list, as well.

# Stop, Look, and Listen

—

*But the Helper, the Holy Spirit, whom the Father will send in my name, he will teach you all things and bring to your remembrance all that I have said to you.*

**John 14:26**

# DEAR Wife,

*Stop. Look. Listen.* Remember hearing that when you were little as grown-ups taught you how to cross the street?

I don't even think about it now when I cross the street. *I just go.* That doesn't mean I don't stop, look, and listen for cars—it means it has become second nature as I have gotten older.

Last summer, while visiting a foreign country where the streets were busy and Vespas buzzed by constantly, I stood multitasking. Attempting to take pictures and cross the street simultaneously, I was inches away from getting flattened when someone grabbed me by the shirt and pulled me to safety.

My multitasking tendencies don't just get me in trouble on the road but in other areas of life as well. I'm inches away from being roadkill in my marriage on a regular basis. How about you? I rush through the day, fail to pause when I get home, rarely look up from my phone to gaze into my husband's eyes, and barely listen to him when I half-ask how his day was. I'm so busy trying to multitask that I put my marriage in danger, and it oftentimes takes something pulling me back to safety for me to see what could have happened.

I'm not engaged; I'm disconnected. I'm comfortable. I'm focused on what I'm doing. I'm not truly listening, acknowledging, or affirming what my husband is saying. I'm basically asking for a crash.

But Jesus arrives at the crash site of disconnection and breathes new life where things seem broken. He cleans up and comes to us with biblical solutions to our brokenness.

At a time when Jesus' closest friends and followers—His disciples—learned that their connection with their leader would be lost, Jesus let them in on important news. He explained to them in John 14:18–19, "I will not leave you as orphans; I will come to you. Yet a little while and the world will see me no more, but you will see me. Because I live, you also will live." He continues to explain: "These things I have spoken to you while I am still with you. But the Helper, the Holy Spirit, whom the Father will send in my name, he will teach you all things and bring to your remembrance all that I have said to you " (John 14:25–26). The disciples were facing the reality that their leader was leaving them alone. Yet, Jesus tells them (and us) that though Jesus was leaving the Earth, the Father would maintain our connection to Him through the Holy Spirit. Life revived and hope restored.

Jesus never left us alone. His fulfillment of the mission of the cross triggered a holy connection through the Holy Spirit living within us. This same Spirit provides us with "love, joy, peace, patience, kindness, goodness, faithfulness, gentleness, self-control; against such things there is no law" (Galatians 5:22–23). The Holy Spirit at work within us breathes life through us toward our spouse by giving us words of love, kindness, and encouragement. Even when we're tired. Or hormonal. Or busy. Or hurt.

Connection doesn't happen by accident. Throughout scripture, we see how Jesus intentionally encouraged people and reminded them to encourage others. Why? Because He knew encouragement develops connection. Encouraging words are in the secret sauce that binds hearts together.

## THE GREATEST CONNECTION DOESN'T HAPPEN IN OUR OWN EFFORT

Whether you are the one who has not intentionally chosen to encourage your husband, or whether your husband hasn't chosen to encourage you, we all have an invitation going forward to create connection by encouraging our husbands. Sometimes we ourselves are the biggest barrier to giving encouragement because we haven't received it first. I want my husband to remind me of how beautiful he thinks I am and tell me how much he loves me. So why is it so hard for me to initiate? I get so caught up in needing to hear words of encouragement that I forget to speak them. Connection is slowly lost. Your husband needs to be acknowledged, and more than that, he needs to be spurred on by the person who is supposed to be his biggest fan: you.

Yet it takes work to engage with one another. And with distractions all around us, it takes even more intention to pause and take notice. Intention requires energy. And when we've spent so much energy on everything and everyone else, our leftover time and energy can be completely depleted.

Friend, I get it. It can be painful to encourage your husband when all you want or need is encouragement yourself. But when you invite the Holy Spirit into your heart, you can let Him guide you and work through you to acknowledge the beautiful parts of the people around you—especially the man you have decided to chase after God with for the rest of your life. Have you invited Jesus into your heart? If you haven't, pray this prayer with me right now:

*Holy Spirit, come. Come live in my heart. Show me how to love like You. Fill me up so I can pour out. Take control of my mind, body, and soul. I surrender my life to You now and forever. I will follow You all of my days and will point others to You. Amen.*

I am praying for the Spirit to fill you and me with words to speak to and over our husbands. I want us to look our husband in the eyes every day and tell him how much he means to us and to God. Easier said than done, right? But we can do it, sister. We can make encouraging our husbands a priority over finishing just one more thing on our to-do list. We can be kind and gentle like Jesus while getting our men ready to go out into the world. We can be our husband's safe place when he can't be strong.

When we let the Holy Spirit sit in the driver's seat and speak through us, we see change happen in our hearts and in our relationships. The reckless driving ceases and the reckless love takes over.

Jesus modeled it for us well when He said to His disciples, "I have said these things to you, that in me you may have peace. In the world you will have tribulation. But take heart; I have overcome the world" (John 16:33). Because of how Jesus encourages us, we can encourage the person He has entrusted to us. Speak truth over your husband and watch your marriage come back to life.

The greatest connection doesn't happen in our own effort. Instead, by relying on the Holy Spirit to fill us and move us, our mouth will speak words of encouragement. When we don't feel like pouring into our husbands, or when we feel too exhausted, that's when we get to rely on the Holy Spirit to work and move within us.

When we arrive home and connect with our husband, we have the opportunity to change the trajectory of his day. It may have been bad before he walked through the door of our home, but with the encouraging power of the Holy Spirit in us, we can stop, look at what's going on within us and around us, and listen to the Holy Spirit so our men land safely in a soft place.

Someone told me once that if a man feels defeated at home, he will feel defeated in the world; if he feels victorious at home, he can conquer the world when he walks out his front door. It's true. Our men need us to fight for them. The world is telling them they aren't tall enough, don't make enough money, and don't drive a nice enough vehicle. We have a front row seat to encourage them and remind them who they are.

We can help them feel victorious through the power of Christ and through the power of our encouraging words.

Your friend,
Kaitlin

**PRAYER:**

*Jesus, we thank You for the gift of encouragement. Thank You for beautifully outlining ways for us to acknowledge our husbands for the wonderful men they are. As wives, we ask You to fill us with Your Spirit and pour out words of life and affirmation when we speak to our husbands. Help us love them like You do. Remind us why we chose them in the first place. Amen.*

**REFLECTION QUESTIONS**

1. How have you seen your words impact your marriage, in positive and negative ways?

_____

_____

_____

_____

_____

2. What are three things you can tell your husband today to encourage him?

_____

_____

_____

_____

3. How does your husband react when you encourage him?

_____

_____

_____

_____

## CONNECT WITH THE FATHER

Spend time now asking God to give you the words that will encourage your husband. Ask Him to speak life into you so you can speak life into those around you. Surrender your thoughts and your tongue so you can glorify Him and strengthen your marriage through the art of kind words. Pray for patience, intentionality, and kindness toward the husband you've been given. Pray for God to mold you into a wife who stops her to-do list, looks around her, and listens to her people.

## CONNECT WITH YOUR HUSBAND

Take a minute now to write your husband a sweet note and put it somewhere he will find it. Then, take the next five minutes to stop and tell him how much he means to you.

# Tearing Curtains

—

*Then Jesus shouted out again, and he released his spirit. At that moment the curtain in the sanctuary of the Temple was torn in two, from top to bottom. The earth shook, rocks split apart, and tombs opened. The bodies of many godly men and women who had died were raised from the dead.*

**Matthew 27:50-52 (NLT)**

# DEAR *Wife*,

I'm pretty much the worst person when it comes to serving others. Being a true servant who is selfless and expects nothing in return? I'd rather not. I have other gifts. You want me to spend time with you? Buy you gifts or encourage you? You bet. I'm there. Die to myself without need for reciprocation? Hmmm. Is there something else I can do? Serving other people just doesn't come naturally to me.

But I married a man whose actual love language—based on Gary Chapman's *The 5 Love Languages*—is acts of service. He makes me coffee, washes the dishes, helps with homework, notices when things fall apart, and sets aside his agenda to put them back together. There are so many times my husband reminds me of Jesus, which can actually make me feel worse about myself. I become very aware of the weight of my sin, my dirt, and my mess. Thank God I am not alone in falling short—and neither are you.

The biggest defining moment of the Christian faith hinges on the ultimate act of service. We aren't talking about morning coffee or math help; we are talking about beatings, humiliation, and finally—terribly—crucifixion. But there is one detail that hits me every single time I read it in the crucifixion narrative. It's subtle, but by no means small.

---

## THE CONNECTION THAT CAN RESULT FROM SERVICE IS ASTONISHING

---

The narrative reads, "At that moment the curtain in the sanctuary of the Temple was torn in two, from top to bottom" (Matthew 27:51 NLT). This wasn't your average living room cotton curtain with trendy designs. This curtain was four inches thick and made out of twisted fine linen with scarlet, blue, and purple thread. The curtain was used as a veil in the Jewish temple, separating the Holy of Holies from the Jewish worshippers. The curtain was placed as a barrier because of sin: it kept God's holiness in and humanity's sin out. But in the moment when Jesus breathed his last? The curtain was torn, top to bottom, in the temple. The curtain was torn so we could enter into the presence of the Most High King. It granted us an all-access pass. No more sacrifices. No more fear. No more trembling. Now, we can boldly approach the throne of grace with confidence and get as close to the King as we want. *Because of Jesus' ultimate sacrifice, nothing can ultimately separate us from Him.*

You and I can usher in this same connection in our own lives, dear one. We can create connection and tear curtains and lay down our lives in our homes. From coffee to conversations, we can serve and create closeness. The connection that can result from service is astonishing. The tiniest act of service can say, *There is no barrier here between you and me. I am humbly laying down some of my life and tearing the veil between us as I do it.*

When we lay down our life, we experience a kind of death. It may be the death of an expectation, of our use of time, or of our agenda. But one thing is sure as we serve: resurrection life is always on the other side of death. God will give us renewed life after we lay it down in service—just like He did with Jesus. That's His upside-down way.

Your friend,
Amy

---

## REFLECTION QUESTIONS

1. What would it look like to open our eyes to serving our spouse?

   _____

   _____

   _____

   _____

   _____

2. As you serve others, what relationship curtains or barriers are you tearing down? Let's be mindful that every act of service creates connection.

   _____

   _____

   _____

   _____

   _____

## CONNECT WITH THE FATHER

Take time to read through the featured passage. Meditate on every word, allowing the ultimate sacrifice given for you to wash over you in a new way. Thank Him for the gift of the cross. Spend time asking God how He wants you to serve your husband in a way that builds connection.

## CONNECT WITH YOUR HUSBAND

Choose to connect with your husband by doing an act of service for him today. Pick a task he typically takes care of in your day-to-day life. Bonus points if it's one he doesn't enjoy doing himself.

# Adjustments in Expectations

—

*And rising very early in the morning, while it was still dark, he departed and went out to a desolate place, and there he prayed. And Simon and those who were with him searched for him, and they found him and said to him, "Everyone is looking for you." And he said to them, "Let us go on to the next town, that I may preach there also, for that is why I came out." And he went throughout all Galilee, preaching in their synagogues and casting out demons.*

**Mark 1:35-39**

# DEAR Wife,

I had just returned home from a four-day trip to an intense women's conference. During the five-hour drive home, all I could think about was pulling into my driveway, unloading my bags, and spending time processing all I had learned.

Unfortunately, life and my family had other plans for me. I opened my door to complete chaos. Boxes lay scattered across the floor, and—of all the unlikely things—restaurant equipment filled my living room. My eyes and mind were overwhelmed at the sight.

While I was gone, my poor husband had the task of moving everything out of the cafe we had just closed. He worked tirelessly in my absence, moving and cleaning. He had eventual plans for all of the "stuff," so my living room was only a temporary home, but the unexpected clutter put a definite halt to my plans.

Instead of heading upstairs to unwind and work on strategic planning for my ministry, I was being asked to help sort through the boxes. *What did I want to keep at the house? What did I want to take to our store in the mountains? What did I want to sell? What did I want to put in storage?*

I was overwhelmed and irritated, but I could see the exhaustion on my husband's face. He looked tired from days of nonstop work. He looked disappointed as he glanced around the room, seeing his hopes for a successful cafe scattered around him, boxed up and marking the end of a dream. He looked as overwhelmed as I was in deciding where all this mess should go. He looked like he needed me.

I'm not the only who has ever felt tugged in two different directions. Jesus Himself was faced with someone else's needs superseding His own. He knew He needed to spend time with the Father, but He was willing to change course when His disciples needed Him. His ability to shift led to opportunities to minister, serving the very people He came to save.

Read what happened in Mark 1:35–39:

> And rising very early in the morning, while it was still dark, he departed and went out to a desolate place, and there he prayed. And Simon and those who were with him searched for him, and they found him and said to him, "Everyone is looking for you." And he said to them, "Let us go on to the next town, that I may preach there also, for that is why I came out." And he went throughout all Galilee, preaching in their synagogues and casting out demons.

Jesus had a plan that morning. He went away to a quiet place for solitary prayer, for time alone to be in communion with His Father in Heaven. It was sacred time.

Yet there were people who were looking for Him. People who weren't concerned with the plans He had made, but instead with their own needs. Jesus could have gotten upset with the change in plans. Instead, He saw their need. Jesus adjusted his expectations and changed the day's course, walking out to the towns to continue the work His Father had given him. How many people benefited from hearing Him that day? How many hearts were reached? Jesus created connection, not only with Simon and His disciples, but likely many others, simply by putting aside His agenda for the betterment of other people.

## *LET'S LEARN TO LOOK AT ADAPTATIONS THE WAY JESUS DID— AS OPPORTUNITIES TO SPARK DIVINE CONNECTION*

Jesus recognized that the end goal was bringing people to the Father, a priority that persuaded Him to put aside His schedule. He knew there was work to do and connections to be made so people felt the love and power of the Father. Knowing this was His ultimate purpose, Jesus responded to His disciples' approach to His prayer time with love.

Likewise, on the day I arrived home to chaos, I badly wanted to have some peaceful alone time. When I stepped over the threshold, however, I recognized that my husband needed me to reassure him that while his old dream may have died, God had given him a new dream and a new opportunity. He needed me to give him support, courage, and love. When my mind recognized that the items on the floor weren't even the real issue, the situation didn't seem like such a rupture to my schedule anymore. Instead, it seemed more like an opportunity for me to be my husband's helpmate, his encourager, his strength and support, and his reassurance.

The enemy wants our unmet expectations to damage our marriage. He wants to cause frustration, resentment, and anger, and he wants to see those feelings grow and fester into something ugly and unmanageable. Yet God wants to use those moments to strengthen and unite us, as we release our rigid expectations and instead choose sacrificial adaptation to change. He wants us to see the bigger picture, recognizing that we are needed and valuable to our families. He wants us to grasp how we have been created for connection, recognizing that the best connection happens when we step outside our wants in the pursuit of someone else's need.

It is so easy to get caught up in our own plans and expectations that we get frustrated when circumstances force us to adjust. Squabbles over disciplining kids, financial burdens, hurtful words spoken out of frustration and anger, or failing to live up to one another's expectations all have the potential to break or build connection in the course of the day. Let's learn to look at adaptations the way Jesus did—as opportunities to spark divine connection.

Your friend,
Betty

---

## REFLECTION QUESTIONS

1. Knowing Jesus made himself available even during intimate, personal time with the Father, how does that influence the way you consider adapting to unexpected needs that arise in your home?

_____

_____

_____

_____

_____

2. If you were to take a thorough, honest inventory of your expectations in marriage and for your husband, would you say they are fair to your spouse and considerate of his needs? Why or why not?

_____

_____

_____

_____

_____

## CONNECT WITH THE FATHER

Take time now to talk with the Lord about your own expectations. How do you approach other people's expectations of your time or priorities? How could choosing to see expectations differently cause shifts in your home or marriage? Bring your heart to the Lord in an honest discussion.

## CONNECT WITH YOUR HUSBAND

Jesus modeled the priority of connecting with people by His ability to be flexible and change His plans. Assess habits and patterns in your life. Are you overwhelmed with the busyness of life? Today, choose one thing to take off your list or say "no" to so that you can say "yes" to more time with your husband. Ask your husband what activity he'd like to do in the extra time you have together.

# The Preparation

And rising very early in the morning, while it was still dark, he departed and went out to a desolate place, and there he prayed. And Simon and those who were with him searched for him, and they found him and said to him, "Everyone is looking for you."

**Mark 1:35-37**

In these days he went out to the mountain to pray, and all night he continued in prayer to God. And when day came, he called his disciples and chose from them twelve, whom he named apostles.

**Luke 6:12-13**

So they took away the stone. And Jesus lifted up his eyes and said, "Father, I thank you that you have heard me. I knew that you always hear me, but I said this on account of the people standing around, that they may believe that you sent me."

**John 11:41-42**

# DEAR *Wife,*

Who doesn't want a stronger marriage? I do—but sometimes I realize I'm causing tension with my husband rather than connecting with him.

My effort to connect often emerges as a barrage of questions: "What time will you be home? Do you know what you want to do about this weekend? Which bill did you say you want to look over before I pay it? Can we have a date night soon, and if so, when?"

My questions are meant to create connection, but they get lost in translation. Me, trying to connect as a couple with other couples. Me, trying to connect as a financial team. Me, trying to connect romantically. Me, trying to connect, even while recognizing that my questions sometimes create more of a disconnect. Sometimes my effort to connect comes across as accusatory: "I told you we needed to let them know by Wednesday. Now it's too late. I wanted to have a date night, but you didn't make a decision, and now I'm busy." No matter how hard I try, my questions fail to produce the results I desire.

I'm talking, but is what I'm really *saying* to my husband making our marriage connection stronger? Sure, life demands questions and the exchange of information. But what am I missing? What can we learn from Jesus about how to truly make stronger connections with people?

In the featured passage, Jesus illustrates how strong personal connections with one another begin with a strong prayer connection to the Heavenly Father. It's easy to wake up and jump into our day without taking time to pray. At the same time, we may be used to giving our husband a piece of our mind when we're upset. But how well are those angry words working to build a strong connection to your husband? If we're truthful, they're not. How might your marriage connection be stronger if you began the day in prayer? When you are upset or have decisions to make, how would talking to God first and praying together as a couple influence the outcome?

Jesus used prayer to build a connection with His Father and with others. We can follow His example to foster connection with our Heavenly Father and with our husband by considering four aspects of Jesus' prayer life:

1. Jesus made His time alone with the Father a priority. Jesus knew that connecting with people's hearts doesn't happen naturally. He made prayer a priority in His day to pave the way for connections with others. Mark 1:35–37 demonstrates how Jesus prioritized prayer. In the early morning, Jesus got up and left the house to pray in a secluded place. Was Jesus able to get up early because His life was uneventful?

Not at all. The previous day and evening was likely filled with teaching and healing. Yet He made His early prayer time with the Father a priority. Jesus chose to make time with God a priority because He knew it would create a connection to His Father that would prepare Him to connect with others. The same holds true for us and our marriages.

2. Jesus prayed before He made decisions. In addition to rising early to pray, Jesus sometimes prayed the whole night. *The whole night.* Why? In the midst of a full schedule, He also had decisions to make, including which men to choose as His disciples (Luke 6:12–13). Jesus took his prayer time seriously because prayer enabled Him to make decisions in line with God's will.

## *JESUS USED PRAYER TO BUILD A CONNECTION WITH HIS FATHER AND WITH OTHERS*

Prayer not only aligns us with God's will, it also aligns us with our husband. If we pray as a couple about commitments, childrearing, purchases, friendships, jobs, and other details, it connects our hearts and minds with one another. If and when things don't turn out exactly as hoped, we know that as a couple, we placed it in God's hands. For instance, Jesus prayed over who to choose for His apostles and chose twelve of them, including Judas. Some might say Jesus made a wrong decision in choosing Judas since Judas betrayed Him. Yet Jesus didn't make a wrong decision. It was in keeping with the Father's will for Jesus to die for our sins. When we pray together as a couple, it defuses fault-finding and builds a stronger connection with our spouse. We know we have approached God, and we trust Him with the outcome.

3. Jesus prayed with other people. Jesus not only made prayer a priority in His day and a factor in His decisions, He also prayed with others. John 11 records the prayer He prayed prior to raising Lazarus from the dead:

So they took away the stone. And Jesus lifted up his eyes and said, "Father, I thank you that you have heard me. I knew that you always hear me, but I said this on account of the people standing around, that they may believe that you sent me." (John 11:41-42)

Why did Jesus pray aloud? He wanted the people around Him to hear and believe that the Father had sent Him to be the Savior of the world. God heard Jesus' prayer and answered it in a miraculous way. God hears our prayers individually and as a couple when we come to Him with our needs. Seeing God answer our prayers strengthens our faith and our marriage connection.

4. Jesus prayed specifically. Jesus prayed with intention. He also encouraged others to pray so that they wouldn't lose heart (Luke 18:1). When the disciples asked Jesus to teach them to pray, He taught them to pray for God's will, for daily bread (food on the table), for the forgiveness of sins, to not be led into temptation, and to be delivered from evil (Matthew 6:9–13). These are specific ways we can pray for one another and for our marriage. John 17:1–26 records additional ways Jesus prayed that show us how we can specifically pray together as a couple:

- that we glorify the Father as a couple
- that our husband would know the Father and Jesus as the one true God
- for the Father to keep us close to Him
- that the Father guard us and our marriage
- that the Father keep us from the Evil One
- that the Father set us apart from the world and place us in the Word of Truth
- that we are one with the Father, one as a couple, and one with other believers
- that our unbelieving husband be saved
- that the Father's love be in us and in our marriage
- that Christ fill us with His Spirit of love, joy, peace, patience, kindness, goodness, faithfulness, gentleness, and self-control

Imagine how these specific prayers for you and your husband will connect you. Jesus' example demonstrates how connection with our husband grows from connection with our Heavenly Father.

We grow and connect with our husband to the degree we grow and connect with God. Admitting that we *desire* a stronger connection with our husband but haven't been faithful to prioritize prayer is a good first step. The second step is to make prayer a priority, as Jesus did.

Your Friend,
Debbie

## REFLECTION QUESTIONS

Take time to reflect on how you start your day.

1. What is your typical morning routine?

_____

_____

_____

_____

2. Do you have a meaningful morning prayer connection with your Father?

_____

_____

_____

_____

_____

3. Do you pray specifically for your husband? Do you pray with your husband?

_____

_____

_____

_____

_____

4. What do you need to do to make prayer a priority so you're more connected to God and your husband?

_____

_____

_____

_____

## CONNECT WITH THE FATHER

Pray: *Heavenly Father, forgive me for the times I've neglected to connect with You in a meaningful way in prayer. Fill me with Your Holy Spirit. Teach me to discern Your voice and walk in Your ways. Help me see my husband through Your eyes and love him with Your heart. Amen.*

Then, share with God how you hope He will work in your husband's heart today.

## CONNECT WITH YOUR HUSBAND

Take the next five minutes to visit with your husband about the importance of a stronger prayer connection.

- Share with your husband how you want to better connect with him.
- Explain that when you connect with God in prayer, it helps you better connect with him.
- Pray with your husband. Ask God to strengthen your marriage.

# It's In The Approach

—

*"While they were talking and discussing together, Jesus himself drew near and went with them."*

**Luke 24:15**

# DEAR Wife,

I was running late again to drop off my daughter for pre-kindergarten. Halfway there, I heard the unmistakable sound of her 2-year-old sister's projectile experience exploding behind me.

"Mommy, it's soooo gross!" exclaimed her sister. *No kidding, honey. Of course it's gross,* I thought to myself.

Frustrated tears pricking the corners of my eyes, I reached for Chick-fil-A napkins to help with the mess. As I did, I heard a small voice utter, "Mama, my tummy no feel good."

In that moment, I felt completely overwhelmed. Why did it feel like I took one step forward and then three steps backwards as a wife and mother? The list of unfinished projects at home flew through my mind. *At least my husband can help me later this evening,* I thought to myself. I called him for a moment of support. His hurried voice on the other end didn't provide the comfort I sought. He reminded me he was heading out of town for four days. I responded with harsh words and hung up the phone without saying goodbye.

I sat in my minivan and cried alongside my 2-year-old. With no local family to assist, I battled anger and frustration toward my husband. *Why was I the only one who took care of the house and the kids? Why wasn't he more supportive?*

Do you ever find yourself in such a place? Near the end of your capacity, badly needing relief, only to realize relief won't be coming? It feels defeating, lonely, and exhausting.

I find it interesting that times of overwhelm and discouragement are the exact situations Jesus used to connect with others. This is illustrated in Luke 24:15–46, when the disciples felt hopeless. They wondered why they had been left alone, seemingly without help. Yet three things stand out about Jesus' approach to His disciples:

1. Jesus entered in when His disciples were most discouraged. After Christ's crucifixion, death, and resurrection, some of His followers walked to a village, talking about Jesus' death and burial while they were on their way. They felt discouraged and wondered how Jesus really could be who He said He was if this was the result. At the moment their spirits reached a new low, Jesus appeared. Why did He appear in that moment? Because the lowest hearts have the most potential to be lifted high. Think about it: when you are at your lowest, aren't those the times you feel most connected to God? A sad, discouraged, exhausted heart has the biggest need for comfort. Jesus knows this, and He wants to provide relief. He does this for you, for me, and for our husbands.

2. Jesus showed great self-restraint, given the circumstances. I can only imagine what Jesus must have been thinking when He appeared before them. After all, He had spent years teaching them and proving to them through miracles that He was the Son of God, preparing them for what would happen. If I had spent my entire life preparing for the greatest act of selflessness and mercy humankind would ever know, only for my friends to doubt it, I would be appalled, hurt, and disappointed. Their doubt might spur me to think, *You're discouraged? You're downcast? Well, I'm hurt that you aren't believing me, trusting me, and listening to me!* Jesus didn't take this approach, however. He didn't appear to them and begin speaking about His holiness or greatness. He didn't attempt to get them to understand His perspective. Instead, He asked questions, listened to their responses, and sought to understand the way they felt.

---

## IF WE ARE TO CONNECT WITH OUR HUSBAND IN THE SAME WAY CHRIST CONNECTS WITH US, WE MUST TRY TO LOOK BEYOND WHAT'S RIGHT IN FRONT OF US

---

On top of that, Jesus purposely waited to reveal His identity. Jesus provided a heart connection first by allowing His friends to share their feelings with Him. He cared more about comforting their downcast hearts than He did about glorifying Himself.

In contrast to my angry reaction toward my husband, Jesus' measured response illustrates how deeply He cared about connecting with the people around Him. Instead of focusing inward, He reached out to the people in His life. He sought to see how they felt, connecting with them on an emotional level.

3. When Jesus revealed His identity, He did it by using God's Word. He interpreted scripture and helped others see the truth by using guideposts that we, as Christians, can rely on in all circumstances. Jesus focused on the word of God, knowing that connecting with the hearts of others is best done when it is rooted in scripture.

4. Finally, Jesus gave them a healthy dose of encouragement and truth. As Jesus sat at the table with His friends, their eyes were opened in awe at the revelation of His presence. In that moment, they realized that what they had heard earlier was now true: the Son of God had risen from the grave. He was who He claimed to be, and He was alive! Their hearts turned from discouragement to delight.

If we are to connect with our husband in the same way Christ connects with us, we must try to look beyond what's right in front of us. Minivan moments have a way of highlighting real-life difficulties and our inability to solve them on our own. After hanging up the phone on my husband and making arrangements for our unexpected day home, I dialed my husband again. Our second conversation helped me realize that my husband hadn't intended to hurt me. He, too, was frustrated because there was nothing he could do to help. Slowing down enough to hear his perspective before allowing my anger to overtake me would have saved us both hours of conflict and frustration. Jesus is always the calm amidst our chaos.

Although feeling discouraged, depleted, or alone is not wrong, our approach to these feelings may lead us down an unhelpful path with our husband. As wives, let's endeavor to see Jesus coming alongside us in all circumstances, just as He walked beside His followers so long ago.

Your friend,
Alynda

## REFLECTION QUESTIONS

1. During times of discouragement, do you turn your attention to God or to something else?

_____

_____

_____

_____

2. Of all the ways in which Jesus interacts with His friends in this encounter, which one strikes you the most?

_____

_____

_____

_____

3. Think about the last few interactions you've had with your husband. How did you stop and listen to his side of the discussion? How do Jesus' interactions differ from your own?

_____

_____

_____

_____

## CONNECT WITH THE FATHER

Reflect on any area in which you are currently feeling discouraged or exhausted. Take a minute to speak to God about your discouragement, inviting Him into your heart. He wants to listen to you and remind you of His great power and comfort.

Next, think about how you would like to interact with your husband when he is feeling discouraged. Ask God to help you respond in a positive way, remembering that with Christ you can make it a reality.

## CONNECT WITH YOUR HUSBAND

Find time to visit with your husband when the kids are in bed or otherwise engaged so that your time together is uninterrupted. Think of a few questions that you could ask your husband that would draw out his heart for a deeper discussion.

Here are some questions to get you started:

- What is something that is going really well at work that you are proud of?
- What is something that is challenging you?
- If you had a few free hours to yourself, what would you want to do with it?
- What is your favorite thing about our relationship right now?

# Choosing To Cherish

One day [Jesus] got into a boat with his disciples, and he said to them, "Let us go across to the other side of the lake." So they set out, and as they sailed he fell asleep. And a windstorm came down on the lake, and they were filling with water and were in danger. And they went and woke him, saying, "Master, Master, we are perishing!" And he awoke and rebuked the wind and the raging waves, and they ceased, and there was a calm. He said to them, "Where is your faith?" And they were afraid, and they marveled, saying to one another, "Who then is this, that he commands even winds and water, and they obey him?"

**Luke 8:22–25**

# DEAR *Wife*,

I just wanted to take a shower. A simple thing, you might think. But with two toddlers who were 23 months apart, I knew it needed to be a quick one. I set them up to play while I hurried through my routine, only to discover they enjoyed the time away from Mom a little too much. As I ran to check on them, I discovered that the younger child had been eating dirt. Potting soil, to be exact. I asked the older child what happened and he responded, "I was pretending Chloe was my dog, and I fed her dirt."

Unfortunately, the dirt-eating episode was just the first of many misadventures. By the time dinner arrived that evening, I felt exhausted by the weight of the never-ending day. Food was dropped on the floor, milk was spilled, and tears were shed. As we painstakingly finished dinner, I began to clean the table and wash the dishes. Standing at the sink with my hands in the dishwater, I felt the touch of my husband behind me as he wrapped his arms around me and began to kiss the back of my neck.

Irritated thoughts flashed through my mind. *Don't kiss me now; grab a towel and get to work. Can't you see I'm busy? I'm so tired. The kids need baths and bedtime. There's so much we need to get done. I'm not in the mood for this.*

---

## THE DISCIPLES' WORRIES WERE NOT SEEN AS AN INCONVENIENCE FOR JESUS, BUT AS AN OPPORTUNITY FOR HIM TO DEMONSTRATE HOW HE CHERISHED THE PEOPLE HE LOVED

---

I was so focused on reaching the end of a tough day with my kids that I overlooked the need to connect with my husband. By remaining focused on the task at hand, I missed the opportunity to take a brief break and soak in the love my husband wanted to provide and the love I could have reciprocated. I forfeited the opportunity to dry my hands on a towel or, better yet, forget about drying my hands while returning the kiss. I lost out on an opportunity to love my husband well because I chose to cherish my to-do list rather than people.

In our featured passage, I wonder how the disciples might have felt if they had awoken Jesus and He had ignored them or told them that He needed to sleep. Jesus could have said, "I have been working all day, and I'm exhausted. Please let Me rest. I don't have time for this." Jesus could have been angry or frustrated that the disciples woke Him up. Instead, Jesus felt compassion. In the middle of a raging storm, a half-asleep Jesus stood up and immediately rebuked the storm. As soon as the words were spoken, the wind ceased and the waves settled.

We see numerous times in scripture where both ordinary and unusual disruptions were welcomed and noticed by Jesus. With the largest to-do list known to man, Jesus was able to pause the proverbial dishes and respond, because connection was what Jesus wanted to achieve. He viewed people, not tasks, as the most valuable consideration.

Thinking back to my husband standing behind me at the kitchen sink, desperate to share his love with me, I wish I had responded more like Jesus responded to His friends. The disciples' worries were not seen as an inconvenience for Jesus, but as an opportunity for Him to demonstrate how He cherished the people He loved.

Now, because of unexpected disease and deteriorated health, my husband is physically unable to stand behind me at the sink, wrap his arms around me, and kiss the back of my neck. I now long for the opportunity to show my husband I cherish him in this way, something I once dismissed. Although this health challenge has robbed my marriage of kitchen sink encounters, it has not stolen my ability to welcome other stolen moments in my life. I am continually learning to be more like Jesus and cherish the person in front of me when disruptions arise. My prayer is this: May I always appreciate the opportunity to dry the dishwater off my hands and take those few moments to cherish my husband.

When our husbands want to have a conversation about a topic we care nothing about or talk to us when we're in the middle of our to-do list, may we not feel inconvenienced. Instead, may we choose to cherish our husbands.

Your friend,
Karen S.

## REFLECTION QUESTIONS

1. How do you respond to disruptions in your life?

_____

_____

_____

_____

2. What are some steps you can take to ensure that you are working on becoming more like Jesus to cherish the ones you love?

_____

_____

_____

_____

## CONNECT WITH THE FATHER

Spend time now with God, reflecting on how He is never inconvenienced by you. Thank God for the personal and consistent access you have to Him.

## CONNECT WITH YOUR HUSBAND

Spend the next five minutes simply investing in your husband. Go to him, ask him if he'd like to spend the next five minutes device-free, and simply be together. While you're together, pay special attention to not interrupting your husband when he speaks, not getting defensive, and intentionally affirming his words.

# Well-Settled Confidence

—

*And calling the crowd to him with his disciples, he said to them, "If anyone would come after me, let him deny himself and take up his cross and follow me. For whoever would save his life will lose it, but whoever loses his life for my sake and the gospel's will save it. For what does it profit a man to gain the whole world and forfeit his soul? For what can a man give in return for his soul?"*

**Mark 8:34-37**

# DEAR *Wife,*

We had just turned left onto the mile-long dirt road leading to my in-laws' farm house when our car quit. After our initial shock, my husband and I both knew what was wrong: it had run out of gas. One week after we bought it the previous year, the gas gauge stopped working. We chose not to fix it, and instead kept track of the mileage to estimate when it needed gas. Sounds like a good plan, right? Except that I'm not a detail-oriented person or good with numbers . . . and it was the car I drove.

So there we sat, frustrated over the empty gas tank. But I also felt confused. I had just checked the mileage and we were fine before we left our house, about 30 miles away. It seemed impossible that it had run out of gas. I shared this with my husband, but he merely shook his head in disbelief. I don't blame him—after all, I had "miscalculated" the mileage on a few occasions and called him to come rescue me. But this time I felt certain that I hadn't miscalculated.

"Weren't you watching the mileage? Didn't you get gas?" my husband asked, upset. "Of course this happened today."

"No, there's something else wrong with it! The mileage was fine; there was only about 20 miles on it. I just looked at it!" I said, attempting to convince him.

He didn't have much more to say, but I sure did. I was furious that he didn't believe me.

"Babe, come on! This is not my fault! I know I saw it, and it was fine. Are you seriously blaming me for this? This is ridiculous! It's your fault we didn't get the gauge fixed anyway—I told you we should. Then we wouldn't be here in the first place!" I yelled.

As someone who likes to think things through and process, my husband got angry with my attempt to push the conversation and blame him, and he got out of the car to start the long walk down to his parents' house to get a gas can.

I sat in the car, watching him slowly make his way down the dirt road. *Ugh,* I thought, *I know this is not my fault. If he would've just fixed this in the first place, we'd have been fine. I didn't do anything wrong! I can't believe him right now.*

Isn't this what many of us do? When our emotions run high, we become hyper-sensitive to any implied criticism. We think, *how dare he point out something I've done when there are so many things he could do differently?* When our husband questions our intentions—whether it's the way we do tasks around the house or our parenting technique—our response is often to fight and push back. We defend ourselves against suggestions and criticism by countering them with the changes we want *him* to make.

I've tricked myself into thinking marriage would be so much easier if my husband were more like me. The result of this thought process is an attempt to make him think like me, act like me, clean like me, and be like . . . *well, me.* When we feel attacked, characteristics we once loved about our husbands while we were dating or at the beginning of marriage become something we can improve. *What great managers and fixers we are,* we think to ourselves. Except there's a problem: most husbands don't want someone to manage and fix them. They want someone to partner *with* them. Dictating equals disconnection.

---

# IT TAKES A WISE WOMAN
# TO CHOOSE CONNECTION
# INSTEAD OF CORRECTION

---

Jesus understood this idea and didn't force people into change. In Luke 8, Jesus traveled to different regions with his disciples. When they arrived in the region of the Gerasenes, Jesus set a man free in a miraculous healing. Yet after the crowds saw how the man had been healed, they were afraid of Jesus and asked him to leave.

This is an integral part of the story, because Jesus was faced with distrust after doing something He knew was both important and necessary. This very scene plays out all the time in marriage, doesn't it? We feel misunderstood, misinterpreted, or falsely accused. And we believe we've done nothing wrong.

I don't know about you, but in those moments, my inner fighter emerges. I am determined to prove how "right" I am and how, if my husband would just change, we'd be fine. It takes a confident woman of Christ to not feel the need to self-protect and justify. It takes a wise woman to choose connection instead of correction.

If I stood behind Jesus as He was questioned and mocked for doing nothing wrong, I would have wanted to cheer Him on: "Aren't You going to tell them what You just did? Tell them why You did it! Stand up for Yourself, Jesus! Don't let them talk to You like that!"

Instead, He said nothing. He didn't push or aggravate them. He didn't make them talk about the situation or declare His awesomeness. Instead, He did what I desire to do more often: He gave them space to process. He was confident enough to let them feel the way they felt, even though He knew it wasn't an accurate picture of His heart. Jesus knew His Father understood Him, which gave Him the grace to be silent.

Jesus sat with me in the car as I was blamed for causing it to run out of gas. He understood. He's been there. He knew I had actually done my due diligence to make sure we had enough gas. But without a real relationship with God at the time, all I knew was that I felt threatened by my husband finding fault with me. In turn, my bid for self-preservation and insecurity kicked into high gear and led to a verbal fight for my husband to believe me. We later realized that my husband had switched the gas mileage tracker over to the oil tracker, and I didn't know. Turned out to be a simple mistake. But looking back, I wish I had known how Jesus was right there, willing to help me in the moment when I felt so threatened.

Ladies, can we learn something from how Jesus trusted God, showed self-restraint, chose to hold His tongue, and decided not to push others to do or think the way He wanted them to? I sure do. I want to be a woman who gives space to my husband to process how he feels. I want to wear humility and be open to how I may be wrong. I want to give my husband freedom to live and not feel as though I'm correcting his every move.

Christ in us will help work this out in our hearts. The Holy Spirit knows that connection doesn't happen through correction; it happens through a well-settled confidence in God. Connection comes in choosing self-restraint and trusting that God will take care of the outcome.

Your friend,
Amanda

## REFLECTION QUESTIONS

1. Do you recognize the tendency to micromanage, push, manipulate, or correct your husband within your heart?

_____

_____

_____

_____

2. How would you like to see Jesus change these impulses and help you to adopt a more trusting, grace-filled, unforced rhythm with your husband?

_____

_____

_____

_____

_____

3. How might your husband's demeanor change as a result of your new attitude?

_____

_____

_____

_____

## CONNECT WITH THE FATHER

Think of moments when you've been angry with God. Think of the times you've pleaded with Him to change your circumstances or fix what seems broken. Consider the times you've doubted God's power or ability. Now, reconsider them—and think about God calmly receiving it all, unchanging in His favor and love for you.

Take time to recognize God's great patience with you. Thank Him for it. Sit with Him and soak in His desire for your heart.

## CONNECT WITH YOUR HUSBAND

Today, list five items that you and your husband struggle to agree on, whether it's a parenting technique or how the dishwasher should be loaded. In two columns, jot down why you think your way is best and why your husband thinks his way is best. Practice seeing things from his point of view.

**Invitation 24**

# Even If

—

*Bearing with one another and, if one has a complaint against another, forgiving each other; as the Lord has forgiven you, so you must also forgive.*

**Colossians 3:13**

# DEAR *Wife,*

I am a soft-spoken, go with the flow kind of gal. My anger isn't easily expressed, and I'm not one that gets easily offended. Unfortunately, when I do get angry, it quickly turns to resentment. My husband often says to others, "Karen doesn't get angry very often, but when she does, she likes to build a house and stay there awhile." Every time I hear this, I cringe. I desire for my husband to tell others how calm and forgiving I am, not how I refuse to forgive. Yet I know I hold tightly to an extended stay at the vacation rental called bitterness, even after my husband has apologized. I replay the offense and the level of hurt it caused. I tell myself that his apology wasn't enough because his level of emotion does not meet my level of hurt.

The truth is, I struggle with truly forgiving and moving past resentment. When my husband has wronged or frustrated me, I choose to hold on to that anger and frustration instead of releasing it. Forgiveness means, "to stop feeling angry or resentful toward (someone) for an offense, flaw, or mistake."[2] Yet this is often a difficult task, especially if the offense is deeply hurtful.

Jesus knew our struggle would be real. In fact, Jesus relates to the deep tension we have in wanting to release hurt and wanting to hold on to bitterness and resentment.

Let's take a minute to follow Jesus to the Garden of Gethsemane. Jesus invites three disciples to join Him in this very intimate place. He asks them to stay awake and remain with Him. When Jesus returns to His disciples, they are asleep. scripture doesn't say that Jesus is offended or hurt. Instead, Jesus converses with His disciples and says in Matthew 26:41, "Watch and pray that you do not enter into temptation. The spirit indeed is willing, but the flesh is weak." In other words, Jesus communicates to them that He knows their heart. He is saying, *Your heart is good, but your flesh is weak, so pray to your Father for help!*

God says the same to us: "I see you want to offer forgiveness to your spouse. I see your heart, but I understand your flesh is weak. So pray."

Deep connection isn't possible without forgiveness, and Jesus doesn't take forgiveness lightly. In fact, forgiveness was Jesus' life mission. When sin entered the world through Satan's deception in the Garden of Eden, humans were separated from a real relationship and connection to the Father. The penalty was a severed relationship with God. When Jesus willingly offered Himself as a sacrifice to bear the weight of our sin and offer forgiveness, our debt was paid, allowing us to experience undivided connection and fellowship with the Lord. Jesus loves us even in our sin, but He loves us too much to leave us there.

Letting go of our resentment by choosing to forgive reinstates relationship, and it offers fresh companionship and deeper intimacy.

I am forgiven even when I throw a laundry basket full of clothes in the air and loudly blame my husband for being insensitive and selfish.

I am forgiven even when, each time my husband wrongs me, I make a list of all the things he has done wrong in the last week.

---

## DEEPER AND MORE MEANINGFUL CONNECTION WAITS FOR YOU AND YOUR HUSBAND WHEN YOU WILLINGLY PUT ASIDE THE BITTERNESS AND RESENTMENT THAT TAKES UP RESIDENCE

---

I am forgiven even when guilt creeps in and makes me feel like I am as good as the trash dumpster down the street.

And, in turn, I'm called to forgive as well.

Sisters, I know I desire to be a wife who doesn't refuse to let go of lingering hurts, and I'm sure you do as well. Our flesh is weak. Our hearts are human and selfish. Forgiveness asks us to put ourselves second. Forgiveness asks us to give up our need to hold our husbands hostage to past hurts. Deeper and more meaningful connection waits for you and your husband when you willingly put aside the bitterness and resentment that takes up residence. All it requires is for you to release the hurt and trust God with the rest.

And so, we pray.

*Father, I pray for the ladies that have just read these words. If our hearts aren't pure, give us a new heart and a new spirit. If we have never experienced Your forgiveness in our own lives, let us stop right now and invite You to live in us and change our hearts to be like Yours. May we give You our sins, knowing that in doing so we can be confident that Your forgiveness is ushered into our hearts and lives. You gave your life so that we could experience forgiveness. It is through accepting Your perfect forgiveness that we can even begin to understand the concept of forgiving our spouse. You didn't utter a war cry on the cross; You cried out for forgiveness for each one of us. Encourage us today. Our hearts desire to forgive, but our flesh is weak. Help us resist the temptation to hold on to anger and have an unforgiving spirit. Give us a willing heart, eager to forgive quickly. Amen.*

Your friend,
Karen S.

—————

## REFLECTION QUESTIONS

1. Are you holding on to specific offenses your husband has committed in the past? If so, what are they?

_____

_____

_____

_____

2. Oftentimes, our unwillingness to forgive is tied to our fear that hurtful actions will be repeated in the future. Can you trust that God is big enough to handle the outcome of your forgiveness?

_____

_____

_____

_____

3. Coming face-to-face with the reality of Christ's suffering so that your own sins could be forgiven, are you willing to release past offenses to Jesus?

_____

_____

_____

_____

## CONNECT WITH THE FATHER

Take time now to evaluate your heart. Refusing to forgive someone who has asked for forgiveness is sin. Pray this prayer from Psalms 139:23: "Search me, O God, and know my heart! Try me and know my thoughts! And see if there be any grievous way in me, and lead me in the way everlasting."

## CONNECT WITH YOUR HUSBAND

Sometimes we need to verbally offer our husbands forgiveness. If God prompts, explain to your husband how you've been holding onto anger and bitterness, but how you desire to release your feelings and offer forgiveness so that nothing stands in the way of your marriage.

Spend the next five minutes with your husband, offering him forgiveness for those things that have placed a barrier in your marriage. Ask him to forgive you in return.

> *A note about ongoing sin: If your husband is currently engaging in ongoing, unrepentant sin in which he does not show a willingness to do whatever it takes to turn from the sin, please seek the guidance of a Christian counselor and consider reading *10 Lifesaving Principles for Women in Difficult Marriages* by Karla Downing.

# Real Relationship

—

*And he asked them, "But who do you say that I am?"*
*Peter answered him, "You are the Christ."*

**Mark 8:29**

# DEAR Wife,

He sat on one bed in the hotel room and I sat on the other. Only a few feet separated us, but it may as well have been miles.

It was our anniversary, and we had done the work of getting a sitter for the kids, the house, and the dogs. We'd packed our bags and taken a little road trip to a room that we'd booked at a beautiful historic hotel. The ride there was quiet. My husband had phone calls to make for work, so I put in my earbuds and listened to an audiobook.

When we arrived, we set down our bags in the room and began to make plans for the two days that spread out ahead of us, just waiting to be filled with romance and excitement. I would make a suggestion that sounded perfect to me, and he'd toss back a look of disinterest. He'd make a suggestion, and I'd give a look implying I'd rather eat dirt.

After volleying ideas for a few minutes, my heart began to throb with a painful thought: *Does he even know me at all?*

That tumbled around in my aching heart until it came out of my mouth as an ugly accusation. As I looked at him sitting on the other bed, obviously feeling frustrated and confused, another thought began to take shape.

*Do you even know him?* Then another. *When was the last time you took the time to try?*

The space between our beds felt cold and distant. The weight of guilt and shame pressing on me felt heavy. I could see I'd blindsided my man with this attack of words. I took a deep breath and asked a question: "If you could do anything over the next two days, what would it be?"

That one little question led to an hour of conversation as we sat side by side on one bed, dreaming out loud about how we'd spend our anniversary trip. I had asked my husband to share his heart with me, and he had gladly complied. In return, I was able to connect with him in a deeper way.

It doesn't play out like this every time. You see, in my marriage, I'm often too self-centered to apply a vital teaching that Jesus modeled time after time in His ministry when dealing with people.

Jesus asked questions that drew out the heart of people to build connection. Did you know that Jesus asked more than 300 questions in the Bible? He didn't loosely throw them around, either. Jesus asked deep questions that encouraged people to share in a way that drew them to Him. People felt like Jesus cared because He took the time to really know them. People felt like Jesus cared because He *did* care.

Often, we can ask questions and then tune out while the other person answers because we are too busy formulating what we want to say next. Or, worse, we don't ask questions at all. We're so set on our agenda or point of view that we forget to even ask the other person what they want or think.

# THAT'S ONE OF THE WAYS JESUS MODELED BUILDING CONNECTIONS IN RELATIONSHIPS

That is what I did on that anniversary trip. I had a perfect weekend in mind, and I hadn't even considered asking my husband what he thought. Instead, I pushed my own agenda, too focused on what I wanted to worry about connecting with him.

Jesus didn't do that. He asked questions to connect to the heart of the person and then He listened, *really listened*, as they answered. That's one of the ways Jesus modeled building connections in relationships. Jesus was after real relationship, not short-term modifications. In fact, Jesus was a master at asking questions because His goal was that His friends—you and I—would experience real relationship with Him.

Sweet wife, I wonder what we might experience in our marriage if we took the time to ask questions that drew out the heart of our husband with the intention of creating real connection. I wonder if we'd experience a rich time of sharing like I experienced on my anniversary trip. I wonder what would happen if we stopped thinking, *Does he even know me at all?* And instead started asking, *What can I ask him to get to know his heart?*

I'd be willing to bet that our marriage would experience a new level of closeness that would surprise us. You see, Jesus knew that we all have a desire to be seen, heard, and known. Through His questions, Jesus let those He interacted with know that He wanted to really see them, hear them, and know them intimately. He did that by asking questions that drew out their hearts to build deep connection.

Let's follow his example, sweet wives. Let's be wives who ask questions.

Your friend,
Bobbie

## REFLECTION QUESTIONS

1. Do you sometimes fall into the same trap that I did, squashing connection by pushing your own agenda on your husband without asking to hear his heart? Explain.

_____

_____

_____

_____

_____

_____

2. In what ways can you better ask your husband questions that let him know you care about him?

_____

_____

_____

_____

_____

## CONNECT WITH THE FATHER

Jesus seeks to know you. He wants real and meaningful relationship with you. He wants your undivided fellowship and conversation. Take time now to talk with God. Share with Him how your day went. Tell Him what you're thinking about or what is on your mind—just simply share your heart with God.

Then, ask God to give you a heart that aspires to see, hear, and know your man. Ask Him to create a desire to listen that outweighs your desire to be heard.

Read through the gospels, the four books of the bible, recording the life of Jesus; Matthew, Mark, Luke and John. Notice how often Jesus asked questions. Look at the ways people responded by pouring out their hearts. Ask God to help you be intentional about creating connection with your husband by asking him questions that will draw out his heart.

---

## CONNECT WITH YOUR HUSBAND

Today, try to learn something new about your husband. Ask him a question about something he enjoys. If it's something you're familiar with or already know about him, keep asking questions about it until he tells you something you haven't heard. Ask him enough questions that you get to the point where you can honestly say, "Wow, I didn't know that!"

# Surrendered Service

Now before the Feast of the Passover, when Jesus knew that his hour had come to depart out of this world to the Father, having loved his own who were in the world, he loved them to the end. During supper, when the devil had already put it into the heart of Judas Iscariot, Simon's son, to betray him, Jesus, knowing that the Father had given all things into his hands, and that he had come from God and was going back to God, rose from supper. He laid aside his outer garments, and taking a towel, tied it around his waist. Then he poured water into a basin and began to wash the disciples' feet and to wipe them with the towel that was wrapped around him.

**John 13:1-5**

# DEAR Wife,

Several years ago, I had a girls' night out planned with my friends. Throughout the year, we would go out to celebrate each other's birthdays, and I always looked forward to getting out of my yoga pants and sprucing myself up to go out for an evening of laughter and fellowship.

On this particular evening, I glanced at the clock and realized my husband would be home soon and I would be free for the night. I put the finishing touches on my hair and makeup, ready to walk out the door as soon as he got home. I planned to pause just long enough to tag my husband "it" so he could take over with the boys and kiss me goodbye.

My husband has always been very supportive of me spending time with my friends, but from the moment he walked in the door, I sensed something was off. Before I bolted out the door, I did the honorary quick chat to find out about his day and learned that it had been a bad day at the office. I could sense his weariness, but was still shocked when he said to me, "Please stay home tonight. I really want you home with me."

My husband didn't want me to miss out on time with my friends, but it was clear he needed me. He didn't need anything in particular, he just wanted me close. I wrestled with wanting and needing a night out with the girls and struggled with whether or not I should stay home. Ultimately, I was faced with the choice to serve myself and go out with my friends or serve my husband by staying home. My heart was heavy as I made the decision to stay home.

I made the selfish choice many times early in our marriage. I put my wants and desires above his needs. However, by the grace of God, I made a better choice that evening: I decided to stay home and care for my husband, not because I had to, but because of my love for him. I wanted to support him. While we didn't do anything in particular that night, I was present for him. It was a small but important gesture that showed the love of Christ in our marriage.

When I spend a hard day working inside or outside of the home, sometimes the last thing I want to do at the end of the day is serve my husband. Our natural inclination is self-serving; it is contrary to our human nature to put the needs of others first. It requires self-control and thinking of others more than ourselves. As wives, that may mean changing our plans to serve our husbands with our presence, by cooking a favorite meal, tidying up before he gets home, picking up his dry cleaning, or initiating a romantic encounter. Loving my husband well sometimes means setting aside my plans in order to show him how much he is loved by serving his needs—without expecting anything in return.

In John 13, Jesus had finished His public ministry and was settling in to spend the evening with His beloved disciples before He faced the cross. Jesus knew His time had come. Soon He would leave this world behind and would be reunited with His Father in Heaven. There was still work to do, yet Jesus took another opportunity to model love. Notice in this verse it says, "Having loved his own who were in the world, he loved them to the end."

---

## *YOU HOLD POWER AND INFLUENCE TO DRAW YOUR HUSBAND'S HEART NEAR TO YOUR OWN AS YOU LOVE HIM THROUGH SERVING HIM, EXPECTING NOTHING IN RETURN*

---

Jesus chose to love the disciples well to the very end. He humbly washed their feet to demonstrate how much He loved them. He assumed the lowly position of a servant not only to share His great love for them but to set an example for them.

We know that Jesus humbled Himself not because He is weak, but rather as a sign of His great authority. Jesus illustrated how to be a servant leader by serving others instead of Himself. He came to serve, not be served. Within a matter of hours, Jesus completed the ultimate sacrifice by laying down His very life for His beloved children.

Wives, I know that giving and serving is hard work. We are tired, busy, and want to have our own needs met. Oftentimes, the idea of doing one more thing for someone else feels impossible. But Jesus, who committed Himself to connection to the Father in all He did, remained continuously fed and filled with perfect love that enabled Him to love others through service. As wives, we can humbly and selflessly serve our husbands by following Jesus' demonstration of His great love for us by serving rather than being served. We can choose to serve without reciprocation because Jesus, the God of the Universe in human form, served the disciples by washing their feet, not expecting anything in return. And He followed this action by humbly surrendering to death on the cross so that we may be forgiven and have eternal life.

Connection isn't built when we choose ourselves. Connection is built through choosing to bless others through surrendered service. Hearts are awed and inspired when loving service is displayed. You hold power and influence to draw your husband's heart near to your own as you love him through serving him, expecting nothing in return.

Your friend,
Misty

## REFLECTION QUESTIONS

1. Jesus lowered Himself and performed the dirty work of washing feet to remind His disciples of His great love for them. What might be a surprising way to show your husband you care for him, love him, and desire to put him before your own wants and needs?

_____

_____

_____

_____

_____

_____

_____

2. How might your marriage look if you decided to reflect the great love of Jesus Christ to your husband?

_____

_____

_____

_____

_____

_____

## CONNECT WITH THE FATHER

Find a few moments to sit quietly with your Heavenly Father, allowing Him to search your heart and reveal any selfish tendencies. Surrender your selfish desires to God and ask Him to burden your heart with a deep love for serving others. Ask God how you can best love and serve your husband in this season of life, looking for creative ways to express love no matter the current state of your marriage.

## CONNECT WITH YOUR HUSBAND

Go to your husband and discuss the following ideas: Forgive me for caring more about serving myself than you. I love you and care more about connecting with you than with being served myself. Follow up the conversation by offering to do a common chore he typically does, thanking him for faithfully taking care of it.

# References

From page XV:

[1] Pritchard, Ray. *An Anchor for the Soul: Help for the Present, Hope for the Future.* Chicago: Moody Publishers, 2000.

From page 118:

[2] Oxford English Dictionary, 'Forgive.' *Oxford English Dictionary.* Oxford University Press, 2014.

# Acknowledgments

To each of our husbands. Thank you for your support, love, and encouragement.
To everyone who helps make the ministry and nonprofit *A Wife Like Me* possible.

To all of our mentors, pastors, and leaders.

To Jesus. You've saved us, freed us, and loved us as we are.

This is all for You.

Amanda Davison
and the *A Wife Like Me* contributor team

*I am thrilled that you have taken the time to grow with God and with your husband. I would love nothing more than to be an encouragement to you in the future.*

*If you are looking for a community to connect with other wives, A Wife Like Me is the place for you!*

*At A Wife Like Me, our mission is to create wives who thrive through an intimate relationship with Jesus Christ by providing beautiful and practical biblical truths and tools.*

*We believe God has placed a high calling on your life and we would love to have you join our community as we share life and learn together.*

*Join with us!*

**Amanda Davison**
**And the *A Wife Like Me* team**

# Contributors

**AMANDA DAVISON** is the wife to a Minnesota farmer, mother of three, and President of *A Wife Like Me*, a nonprofit. She is an author, speaker, and also serves on staff at her local church. Amanda is relentlessly sharing how her education in counseling and God's word changed her life and marriage.

**ALYNDA LONG** is the founder and editor of the ministry Faith Beyond Fear. In addition to blogging, editing, writing, and speaking, she serves as a lay leader in her church's recovery ministry. She thrives on Jesus, coffee, books, friendship, and chocolate. Alynda lives in Texas with her husband and children.

**AMY SEIFFERT** has been writing, teaching, and speaking on staff with Cru for over 17 years and is currently the Director of Outward Movement at Brookside Church. She has been married to Rob since 2001, and they live in Bowling Green, OH with their three children Robby, Olive, and Judah.

**BETTY PREDMORE** is an author, speaker, blogger, and ministry leader. She has published two devotionals: *Pondering Virtue* and *Whispered Grace*. In addition to *A Wife Like Me* Betty has also contributed to *Southern Faith Magazine* and *Aspiring Woman Magazine*. She also runs her own online encouragement ministry called *Mom-Sense*.

**BOBBIE SCHAEPERKOETTER** is a writer, speaker, teacher, YouTuber, community builder, and an empowerer of women at Bobbieschae.com. She makes her home in Jefferson City, Missouri, with her hubby and two boys. Bobbie believes that women need to do relationships and ministry in a counter cultural way that honors God.

**DEBBIE TAYLOR WILLIAMS**, founder of P.R.A.Y. with Passion Across the Nation Conference, is a popular Bible teacher, faith columnist, blogger, and speaker. She's authored seven books, including *Pray with Purpose, Live with Passion* and *Prayers of My Heart*. She and Keith have two children and five grandchildren.

**ELIZABETH OSCHWALD** is a writer, teacher, and single mama coach. Having walked through divorce, single motherhood, remarriage and blending families, she loves to encourage women who have found themselves on the messy side of grace. She and her husband enjoy life in their Illinois farmhouse, along with their seven kids.

**KAITLIN CHAPPELL ROGERS** is a writer, speaker, and dreamer passionate about pointing people to the Truth. When she's not writing, she's either catching up with friends and family over coffee or traveling with her husband! She writes at kaitlinchappellrogers.com and you can connect with her on social media at @kaitlinchappellrogers.

**KAREN FRIDAY** is a pastor's wife passionate about women's ministry, speaking, and sacred callings. Known as Girl Friday in the writing and blogging world, she founded *Hope is Among Us* at KarenGirlFriday.com. Her family includes two grown children and two grandchildren. Fond of "TGIF," they owe Monday an apology.

**KAREN SMITH** blogs at www.karenkaysmith.com where she empowers others to live transformed. Karen is a regular contributor for *A Wife Like Me*, has been involved in women's ministry for many years leading small groups, making hospital visits, organizing retreats, and encouraging the hearts of women in Madison, Alabama.

**KARLA DOWNING** is an author, speaker, teacher, marriage and family therapist and founder of ChangeMyRelationship.com. Karla's passion is to see individuals, marriages, and families set free from dysfunction and scriptural misunderstanding. Her messages provide practical solutions based on biblical truths that bring balance and clarity to life and relationship issues.

**KRISTIN MILNER** is happily married to her pastor hubby Tim, and together they have three beautiful girls. Her family felt called to move back to the South where they started Essential Church, a church for people who no longer thought church was for them. Follow her stories at www.kristinmilner.com.

**MISTY PHILLIP** is passionate about helping women overcome challenges in life. Seeking Jesus, studying the Word and growing in grace. She is the author of *The Struggle is Real: But so is God Bible Study*, host of the By His Grace Podcast, sought after speaker and blogger at MistyPhillip.com

**NATALIA DRUMM** is a wife, mother of 3 boys, lover of Jesus and Bible study teacher. Her and her husband have a heart for building strong marriages. Natalia loves women's ministry and leading people to study the Word of God. Follow her on social media and her website: www.nataliadrumm.com.

**SARAH GERINGER** writes about Finding Peace in God's Word at sarahgeringer.com and is a freelance writer, author and artist. Her first traditionally published book, *Transforming Your Thought Life: Christian Meditation in Focus*, will publish with Leafwood Publishers in October 2019. She lives in Missouri with her husband and three children.

**SHANNON GEURIN** has a messy story that's been redeemed by an extravagant Jesus. She's a writer and speaker but Wife and Mom first. Shannon serves an actively engaged community of women who are RISING UP through their circumstances. You can find her at www.shannongeurin.com, and on FB and Instagram.

**SUSAN WILDER** encourages women to seek God first so we overflow with His joy and peace to others. Susan is married to Frank, and they have three married daughters and one son, while also being Mimi to four grandboys. Susan serves as Women's Ministry leader in Louisville, Kentucky.

Made in the USA
Middletown, DE
14 July 2019